# ADVERTISING AND CULTURE

*Premiere* by Stuart Davis (1892–1964), the American artist, enshrines the words of advertising. Oil on canvas, 55x50 in., 1957. Los Angeles County Museum of Art, Museum Purchase, Art Museum Council Fund.

# ADVERTISING AND CULTURE

## Theoretical Perspectives

Edited by
# MARY CROSS

Westport, Connecticut
London

**Library of Congress Cataloging-in-Publication Data**

Advertising and culture : theoretical perspectives / edited by Mary
   Cross.
      p.   cm.
   Includes bibliographical references and index.
   ISBN 0–275–95351–3 (alk. paper)
   1. Advertising—United States.   2. Popular culture—United States.
   3. Communication in marketing—United States.   I. Cross, Mary.
   HF5813.U6A6177   1996
   659.1'042'0973—dc20          95–26518

British Library Cataloguing in Publication Data is available.

Library of Congress Catalog Card Number: 95–26518
ISBN: 0–275–95351–3

First published in 1996

Praeger Publishers, 88 Post Road West, Westport, CT 06881
An imprint of Greenwood Publishing Group, Inc.

Printed in the United States of America

The paper used in this book complies with the
Permanent Paper Standard issued by the National
Information Standards Organization (Z39.48–1984).

10 9 8 7 6 5 4 3 2 1

**Copyright Acknowledgments**

Excerpts from lyrics and dialogue in the General Electric "Tapestry" commercial
are reprinted by permission of BBDO New York.

The story "Gallery" by Stephen-Paul Martin is reprinted by author's permission
from *The Literary Review*, Summer 1990.

To our students

# Contents

# Acknowledgments

We would like to acknowledge and thank all of those who assisted in the preparation of the camera-ready version of this book, especially Walter Cummins, without whom it would not have been possible at all. His advice and expertise were invaluable in the computer typesetting, designing, and printing of this text. For expert help with the index, we are indebted to Martin Green.

For the conversion of discs, scanning of manuscript, and other technological help, we thank Lisa Stadler, David Mooney, Liz Wismann, and Parag Modi. And for help in dozens of ways, we thank Chris Napolitano, who always manages to make the work of the English and Communications Department go smoothly.

We are most grateful to our editors Nina Pearlstein, Maureen Merlino, and Kim Hastings at Greenwood Publishing Group for their excellent guidance as we prepared this book.

# Introduction

Churning out its daily dose of headlines and come-ons, the media circus of American culture roils on to the millennium. We ready ourselves for the supposed apocalyptic moment when the 20th century becomes the 21st and we will all be turned into pumpkins or geeks or cyborgs. Many people think we are on the verge—or right in the middle of—radical transformations in the way we live and apprehend the world. Some call it postmodernism, others the end of history. Still others claim we cannot possibly give a name to something we hardly understand yet.

At the very least, it seems, the print world we have known and loved is in the process of being transformed into electronic blips, a cyberspace of hypertext and Internet where sound, word, image, and millions of people intermingle. The potential for advertising, and for advertising revenues, has corporate America falling all over itself to go on-line and extend the reach of advertising's pervasive public discourse to this emerging cybernation of consumers.

That is just business as usual in the United States, home of the Yankee peddler and the traveling salesman, the Super Bowl and the award-winning 15-second TV commercial. Advertising is, after all, indigenous to American culture. Indeed, this book argues that advertising, in its omnipresent public words and images, plays a determining role in creating that culture. Most arguments, particularly those from the advertising industry itself, take the opposite approach: Ads are mere mirrors, just reflecting culture, not creating it.

Yet our experience tells us otherwise. Growing up, some of the first words we speak are brand names; some of the first rhymes we remember and first tunes we hum are straight out of commercials. We learn from watching television that buying things is supposed to make us happy, and we learn to shop, participating in the system by choosing and consuming products. Half-consciously, even cynically, we let commercials modify our behavior and construct our identity as they teach us how to act and how to dress, what to eat and what to drive. We thought Andy Warhol was just kidding when he painted all those rows of Campbell's Soup cans, but pop art was about the ads and the brands rather than the soup, and it ruthlessly made clear the culture of brand names and hype we took for granted. Advertising has become our culture's primary visual reference, as one art critic has lamented.

Certainly American advertising has long attracted the attention of scholars as a rich repository of our cultural attitudes and values. This volume is a collection of scholarly essays that explore the ways advertising has influenced American culture at the end of the 20th century. Through the lens of poststructuralist and cultural studies theory, the authors examine print and TV advertising to show how it has shaped our culture with its grand narratives. Each essay in its own way both affirms and questions advertising's premises, attempting to understand its influence in the light of new theory and to probe the ideologies and the culture it sustains. In addition, the essays have the purpose of helping to define a cultural moment, one called, for lack of a better name, postmodernism. The subject matter of the essays ranges from defining advertising as myth to accounting for its role in shaping postmodern culture, from examining such contemporary issues as sexism, racism, and cultural stereotypes to addressing aesthetic questions of word and image. The emphasis on TV advertising is deliberate; the power and ubiquity of television make it the best medium for advertising ever invented.

In "Reading Television Texts: The Postmodern Language of Advertising," we take a close look at the discourse of advertising as it transforms the language and culture of our fin–de–siècle time, turning words into images and dissolving reference in order to tempt us with new and more seductive meanings.

At the end of the 20th century, sexism and racism remain major issues, and, troublingly, advertising continues to perpetuate some of the stereotypes, as Elise Salem Manganaro shows in her essay, "When Foreign Sells: Exotica in American TV Ads of the Eighties and Nineties." Advertising's "simplified notions of Otherness" and the exotic, she argues, are used as romantic, sanitized images to lure American consumers to products while at the same time playing on fears about the unknown and caricaturing the foreign.

In "Some Versions of the Pastoral: Myth in Advertising; Advertising as Myth," Martin Green discusses advertising's offer to "recuperate the originary world" for us as it evokes the pastoral past and sells us nature along with a car or a hotel room. If the recuperation of origins was the ultimate quest—and failure—of belated modern culture, advertising claims to triumph, Green says, by invoking imagery of the pastoral. Yet, he concludes, such a project remains unfulfilled, even unfulfillable.

Harry Keyishian argues in "'We Bring Good Things to Life'/ 'We're Always There': The AdWorld of GE" that companies like General Electric are heavily invested in showing themselves as benign public benefactors with humane goals that will benefit everyone from their workers to humanity as a whole. The elaborate

Introduction xiii

process of creating such an image reveals how much Americans want to believe in it.

Using examples from literature and the arts, some authors investigate advertising's appropriation of literary techniques to influence the consumer. Walter Cummins, in "Love and Liqueur: Modernism and Postmodernism in Advertising and Short Fiction," describes the way narrative technique shapes—or fragments—a sales message to manipulate the reader-consumer's response. His essay defines both the modern and the postmodern forms of advertising, comparing them to modern and postmodern fiction.

Roger Koppl, in "Man Has Fallen and He Can't Get Up: An Essay on Postmodernism and Advertising," looks at advertising's promises to save us; it offers us pseudo–redemption in the form of products. Preserving us perhaps from a worse fate or a false prophet in our quest for salvation, advertising trains us in our role as consumers to "just buy it." Ultimately, as Koppl, an economist, subversively suggests, this is an excellent method of political control.

In "Burroughs and Advertising: Fractured Language, Fractured Time, Fractured Image as the Universal Language," Michael B. Goodman shows how William S. Burroughs, author of *Naked Lunch,* threw out narrative altogether to give fiction—and advertising—a distinctly new structure, predating the jump-shifts and juxtapositions of MTV by several decades and influencing the audience in a visceral rather than intellectual way.

Analyzing the way advertising imagery reinforces concepts of gender role and behavior, Judith Waters and George Ellis reveal the stereotypes that populate print and TV ads in "The Selling of Gender Identity." Advertising uses its own reductive images for the portrayal of gender, and consumers tend to incorporate these in their own self image.

Donald W. Jugenheimer takes a positive view of advertising's influence on culture in "Advertising as Educator," showing how its strategies of instruction and persuasion work and how such strategies might invigorate teaching and learning in the classroom.

Chester St. H. Mills and Rebecca A. Chaisson, in "The Betrayal of the Media," discuss the way advertising exploits racial and gender imagery and consigns groups of people to view themselves as an underclass. Dealing in stereotypes, advertising betrays these groups to commerce and the class structure, they argue.

All of these essays are the result of an unusual collaboration among scholars of different disciplines, including English, Communications, Psychology, Sociology, and Economics. The variety of perspectives on advertising presented here will, we hope, offer some new ways to understand the vibrant and provocative discourse that surrounds all of us every day of our lives, suggesting new directions for examining the culture it creates.

# 1

# Reading Television Texts: The Postmodern Language of Advertising

*Mary Cross*

Advertising is, no question, the language of capitalism. Its "buy me" message on everything from designer jeans to billboards bombards the average American more than 1500 times a day. No one who watches television, listens to a radio, drives a car down a highway, shops the mall, or reads a magazine or newspaper can ignore this language of the marketplace, where words of one syllable pitch promise in sound bites of desire: "Just Do It"; "This Bud's for You"; "Where's the Beef?"

Welcome to the culture of daily life, American style, where experience has been reduced to "a series of pure and unrelated presents," as Fredric Jameson describes it (76), a collage of short-take messages cajoling us to find in consumption the answer to whatever is ailing us at the moment. And, it would seem, there *is* something ailing us as, under pressure of advertising's cacophonous language, "the world seems to lose its depth and . . . become a glossy skin, a stereoscopic illusion, a rush of filmic images without density" (Jameson 76–77).

If postmodernism can be understood as the cultural logic of late capitalism, the logical move of market into culture as Jameson contends (92), the language of advertising in league with TV has, I would argue, provided its major premises. "Culture is a creation of speech," as Neil Postman observes (10), a product of the unique human faculty of language; as Foucault showed, a system of discourse can be a code for the legitimation of a social order and its control. The discourse of advertising, breeding "an environment of philistinism, of schlock and kitsch" (Jameson 54), of fragmented image and truncated statement in its rapid-fire, terrorist assault on our senses, has in effect re-created our culture, transforming both the outer landscape in which we live and the inner one, consciousness, by which we try to make sense of what is going on. In both spaces, there has been an immense shift in sensibility, one that advertising has helped to create through the most perfect medium ever invented for the wholesale marketing of culture, television. Technology *is* ideology, without words, as Postman points out (86).

Indeed, as the virtual "command center" of our culture, TV promotes consumption to keep markets buoyant, spawning through advertising its own brand of consumption rhetoric.

Profoundly American, the language of advertising insists upon speed, enshrining the perpetual present in repetitions worthy of a Gertrude Stein, giving in its incantation a material presence to words as it pries them loose to code a commodity culture.   In disdaining past and future, in reifying speed, in presenting a fragmented, ideologically loaded picture of reality, advertising not only replicates the social moment, as Jameson claims, but also has in large measure assisted at its creation.  The social moment of postmodernism is thus a kind of inevitable product of this pervasive public language, one that coats reality with glossy surface and asks us not to think, closing off the universe of discourse through one-dimensional words and a one-way communication that leave us panting, but passive, allowed to participate in the system only as consumers. Pandering to our base appetites or desires, advertising in the pornography of its excess eroticizes words into images and collapses individual consciousness into equations of money and psyche.

Seemingly the language of advertising has no depth, offering a hyped-up surface to be seen that supplants logic and even language itself as images spread and assault linearity.  Yet it draws us in with disjunctions of wordplay and image to reach subliminally into dimensions of the forbidden, training us to new attachments.  This public sign system, in making meaning for products, has created a new world view,  offering utopia in a narrative of going out to buy, a simulacrum of the world that drives us to products as substitutes for experience.  Content in our cool inertia,  we have allowed brand names, as Todd Gitlin observes, "to become the furnishings of our cultural 'home'" ("Hip-Deep in Postmodernism" 35).

"Promising relief from feelings of unreality," advertising from the beginning connected its strategies with those offering therapeutic help, "manipulating feeling rather than presenting information," as Jackson Lears argues (21). Further, Lears says, advertising exacerbates those feelings "by hastening what the French sociologist Henri Lefebvre has called  'the decline of the referentials'—the tendency, under corporate capitalism, for words to become severed from any meaningful referent," lending  the world of advertising "an Alice-in-Wonderland quality" (21).

Indeed, peeling verbal signs off their traditional associations in attention-getting wordplay and fragmented syntax, advertising employs a kind of linguistic vandalism to create its spurious surface of language games, appropriating words for use in a realm somewhere between truth and falsehood, and motivating the signifiers to serve its own purposes—motivating the customer.  Who had heard of halitosis, tired blood, or ring-around-the-collar before adspeak made them part of the common language?  Who had cared about oat bran or even cholesterol counts until advertising built them into its perennial come-on of health claims?  Like the ubiquitous black-and-white bar code on everything from magazines and cake mix to Christmas ribbon and raw meat, language is coded and recoded by advertising to speak in its own marketplace tongues.[1]  Advertising has always played language games; its own special game is connotation, raising the stakes on words to enlarge their suggestiveness by shifting contexts (puns) or making new equations (metaphors) or changing their spelling (neologisms). Indeed, advertising's game is to turn language into logo, not logos, into glamour, not grammar, moving it out of the rational to the non-proposition of the figural, the visual, where images like those of our dreams can take command of consciousness to promote that great big marketplace dream of material happiness, the American one.

## BAUDRILLARD'S HYPERREAL

If language, like money, has always been thought to stand in for a signified amount of real world value, symbolic like cash over the counter in exchange for the real, advertising has emptied out the signifiers so as to project its own fantasies on them. In the telelanguage of advertising, the alphabet is transformed, like money, into electronic impulses. Like money, words become plastic, credit cards full of promise, eliminating the need for the real—money or meaning—or even considerations of cost. Like holograms, they shimmer, floating signifiers cutting a stylish typographical figure on the screen or page or package and intoned ingratiatingly in voice-overs that speak directly to the id. Jean Baudrillard contends that as advertising and the media privilege the signifier and dissolve reference, the postmodern presents a crisis of representation. As he says, "All of Western faith and good faith was engaged in [a] wager on representation: that a sign could refer to the depth of meaning, that a sign could *exchange* for meaning and that something could guarantee this exchange" (170). If "representation starts from the principle that the sign and the real are equivalent (even if this equivalence is Utopian, it is a fundamental axiom), conversely simulation starts from the Utopia of this principle of equivalence, *from the radical negation of the sign as value*, from the sign as reversionand death sentence of every reference" by enveloping "the whole edifice of representation as itself a simulacrum" (170). That is, as Baudrillard defines it, the strategy of the "hyperreal," substituting signs of the real for the real itself and "liquidating all referentials" (167). Signs—especially those, I would add, in the hands of advertising—"are more ductile material than meaning, in that they lend themselves to all systems of equivalence . . . providing all the signs of the real," but "short-circuiting" its vicissitudes. "Divinely irreferent," signs and images thus "*play at being* an appearance," "masking the absence of a basic reality—or bearing "no relation to any reality whatever: it is its own pure simulacrum" (170).

To this crisis of representation, the language of advertising—and of television—has contributed mightily. Liquidating the referentials to establish their own systems of equivalence, in tandem they motivate the signifiers to create a mutant public language that masks the absence of a basic reality. Mark Poster, in *The Mode of Information,* gives a Baudrillardian description of how it works:

The ad takes a signifier, a word that has no traditional relation with the object being promoted, and attaches it to that object. The ad constitutes a new linguistic and communications reality. These floating signifiers derive their effects precisely from their recontextualization in the ad. Extracted from an actual relation between lovers, romance or sexiness increases in linguistic power. In the ad, sexy floor wax is more romantic than a man or woman in an actual relationship. This surplus meaning . . . derives from the unique linguistic structure of the ad. Romance in the floor-wax ad is constituted by words and images that are not found in daily life. An attractive man abruptly appears in (penetrates into) an ordinary kitchen while an average woman futilely scrubs away using the wrong product. The very impossibility of the sexy man making his appearance in the kitchen as he does (he pops into the picture, for example, by virtue of a careful splice of the videotape) sets the ad apart from representation and scientific logic. The cartoon-like appearance of the man registers the image as fantasy, a fantasy of Prince Charming but a Prince Charming who exists not in books of fiction, not in remote fairy tales, but in an image of a kitchen very much like one's own. Johnson's floor wax now equals romantic rescue. The commodity has been given a semiotic value that is distinct from, indeed very out of phase with, its use value and its exchange value. The very "senselessness" of the relation romance=floor wax is a condition of its communications meaning. (58)

"The ad shapes a new language, a new set of meanings (floor wax/romance) which everyone speaks or better, speaks everyone," Poster observes, summarizing Baudrillard (58).

This is a language we cannot refute. It uses no argument—its claims are not logical, but visual. Adspeak's new equations take language to the figural, to images and dreamscape where advertising would like it to be, registering on the unconscious. It is this devaluation and substitution of signs, the "strategy of the hyperreal," by which advertising, in league with TV, transfigures the word virtually into Freudian dream—or nightmare—image. This emptying out of language is at the heart of the paradigm shift we are calling postmodernism, a crisis of representation that leads to "new structural dimensions introduced by the source of information," which, as Poster says, "critical social theory cannot grasp" until it takes account of the "language effect of ads" (59). Indeed, as Postman observes, TV commercials have now become "an important paradigm for the structure of every type of public discourse" (126).

## LANGUAGE AS CULTURE

But even without TV, adspeak is designed to acculturate its subjects. I speak here as a practitioner, a former advertising copy chief. I am among those Daniel Bell defines as the "cultural mass" who mine culture for the buzz words that will capture the attention and increase the vulnerability of the public to manipulation by mass media. Extracting these signifiers from the social, I and others redeployed them in media, that "decoupage" mode of signification where, in an irony of late capitalism, words like "free" and "new" are still the single most effective words in adspeak's lexicon. Drawing on the efficient Anglo-Saxon adspeak—from which

George Orwell predicted Newspeak would come—trades in concrete nouns and imperative verbs, fragmented sentences, clichés, puns, and parodies of speech rhythms, all delivered in a quasi–Crazy Eddie style. Its discontinuities and gaps, like pornography, excite us; it draws us in by saying "You can do anything you want to do," but it gives us nothing, short-circuiting the realization of desire and yanking away the object to leave us in naked need, cravenly alone. Driven by the discourse of advertising, we remain unsatisfied, suspended. Yet adspeak denies us even our negativity; it is happy talk, coded to take over reality with a logic of its own. TV, as a machine of consumption, has created the context for this mutant language, accelerating the process by which signs degenerate into image and words to mere typography. In its bid to replace a print technology, TV does not use very much of it; words seem vestigal, by-products of the visual in electronic communication, where a word on the screen must be recognized (though not necessarily understood) in the "instancy" of its 3.5-second moment (Postman 130). The word has become optical, even opaque, occupying space rather than seen through for meaning, and designed in its sans serif Helvetica or Futura typography for speed reading like a headline. Indeed, on the TV screen, it exists only in the act of reading. [2]

If typography in its day arrested linguistic drift, now TV has virtually arrested the linguistic itself in image as a form of commodity, an optics of language that overwhelms grammar and logic. In a print technology, words have to fit the space; in an electronic technology, they have to fit the time, and images are faster—and more real—than sentences and paragraphs. TV cannot handle complexity, as Postman comments: "It is the nature of the TV medium to suppress the content of ideas to accommodate the requirements of visual interest. TV is at its best when substance of any kind is muted and emptied out of reference" (92, 116). Thus TV's adspeak, its slogans and jingles, is more like haiku than discourse. Indeed, in undermining logic with emotional appeals, adspeak pulls the rug out from under any test of truth. There is thus a kind of "Vanna effect" in the new visuals of language, as Marshall Blonsky might say, where, laminated for our perception, it presents itself as a surface we can read into whatever we wish.[3] Stuart Ewen remarks in *All Consuming Images* that "[i]n countless aspects of life, the powers of appearance have come to overshadow or to shape the way we comprehend matters of substance" (159). Information and ideas are in large measure communicated these days in advertising by their style and appearance, a manipulated surface. In such a context, even words seem to be material objects, a privileging of the signifier and the visual, not the signified. As Jameson says:

In normal speech, we try to see through the materiality of words . . . towards their meaning. As meaning is lost, the materiality of words becomes obsessive, as is the case when children repeat a word over and over again until its sense is lost and it becomes an incomprehensible incantation . . . . A signifier that has lost its signified has thereby been transformed into an image. (66)

The resulting "isolated, disconnected, discontinuous material signifiers which fail to link up into a coherent sequence" contribute to the peculiar, "schizoid" sense of time and identity that Jameson sees as characteristic of our postmodern era, condemning us "to live in a perpetual present with which the various moments of [our] past have little connection and for which there is no conceivable future on the horizon" (65).

TV's own code of electronic signals contributes to this effect, limited as it is to "basically one degree of complexity," as Joshua Meyrowitz notes (76). While print offers more variables, its linear structure and segregation of information have been broken down by the electronic media, Meyrowitz observes (79). TV has to reduce ambiguity, narrow its symbols (a picture, after all, when you are talking to the id, is worth a thousand words), and democratize language so it is available to all: TV's access code must be accessible. Reading takes too long. It is not an all-at-once activity, and it takes practice. TV and advertising, however, have found instant access by using a very literal level of words, appealing to emotion, discouraging thought. Using grammatically simple, short, or partial sentences and few adjectives or adverbs, eliminating conjunctions, and using descriptive, concrete nouns, advertising has created a public language to reach out and touch "mass man."[4] TV, as Meyrowitz notes, has "homogenized" the public (87), merging audiences in an "equalization" process that cancels contexts and "blurs the isolated situations fostered by print"—time, space, sex, education, race, religion, class—"into a relatively similar informational world" (92). Like Marshall McLuhan's global village and Guy Debord's society of spectacle, such homogeneity is the result of television's pervasive power. Thus, too, the boiled-down public language of adspeak leaves no one out. It offers a "restricted" code, like that of the lower-class speakers categorized in Basil Bernstein's study of class-specific modes of speech, "A Public Language: Some Sociological Implications of a Linguistic Form." Marked by "grammatically simple, syntactically poor" sentences, which do "not facilitate the communication of ideas and relationships which require a precise formulation" (315), such a code is characterized by "a low causal level of generality" aimed at "maximizing the emotive rather than the logical impact" of language (311). Thus, it allows for "a grasp of the here and now," not "an analysis or transcendence of the social context," as Claus Mueller observes and it "reinforces the cohesion of a group that shares a specific code" (432). Yet like the language of advertising, as I would argue, it also deprives its speakers even as it conditions their perceptions, narrowing their ability to conceptualize and discriminate and "rendering their condition more acceptable to them" by immunizing them "from perceiving alternatives" (Mueller 432–33). Like the violent and simple language of adspeak, the emphasis is on discontinuity, particularity, and the ephemeral. It is the language of the characters in the movie *Goodfellas*, who fight over the meaning of a single word because they take its connection to reference so literally. And it is the language of Thomas Pynchon's "Thanatoids" in *Vineland,* who are addicted to TV, their eyes glued to the Tube, and who must go to Tubal Detox to be deprogrammed.

## THE POSTMODERN MOMENT

In the advertising of the nineties, the words of a print culture are in the process of being displaced, made marginal, captive to image. As evidence that words as meaningful signs are on the way to becoming cultural artifacts, art appropriates their forms, as far back as Cubism's and Surrealism's use of words as image, and as recently as Barbara Kruger's "word salads" and Jenny Holzer's electronic posters incorporating words as public "art" and as sharp parodies of advertising's public language. TV commercials portray the verbal as nostalgia for an older art form; David Lynch's ads for Calvin Klein had only one printed word in them, the logo "Obsession," yet quoted freely in voice-overs from the art-speech of Ernest Hemingway and Scott Fitzgerald, Gustave Flaubert and D.H. Lawrence in order to equate their words with the images of shaving lotion that fill the screen.[5] The lip-synching of Milli Vanilli and even of George "read-my-lips" Bush spoke volumes about the role of image as a first-level method of communication—lip-reading as a mode of signification requiring a "sleight-of-eye" to understand.

As Barbara Kruger told one critic, her art of words and pictures is about giving back meaning:

There is an accessiblity to pictures and words that we learned to read very fluently through advertising. . . . But that's not the same as really making meanings. . . [television is] basically not about making meaning. It's about dissolving meaning. To reach out and touch a very relaxed, numbed-out, vegged-out viewer. (qted. in Mitchell 447)

TV, Kruger says, is *about* meaninglessness through media accessibility, "about, as Baudrillard has said, 'the space of fascination,' rather than the space of reading" (qted. in Mitchell 447). If the media have made things meaningless through accessibility, Kruger—like her contemporaries Cindy Sherman, Sherrie Levine, and Jenny Holzer—says she is at work to recuperate the "leased and mortgaged" words and images of the postmodern. In that postmodern moment, we do seem to live in a pagan, "vulgarized plurality," a "bricolage" culture something like that experienced by "a remote-control-equipped viewer 'zapping' around the television dial" (Gitlin, "Postmodernism" 355, 347) or Pynchon's Tubefreek, a creature hooked on MTV and living in Baudrillard's hyperreality, where the real is no longer the real and words are just another surface.

If "modernism tore up unity," Gitlin says, "postmodernism has been enjoying the shreds," in an "utter dispersion of voices" mixing "levels, forms, styles," relishing "copies and repetition," and taking "pleasure in the play of surfaces . . . ricocheting . . . and reverberating" to "exhaustion" on everything from Michael Graves's architecture and Warhol's Brillo boxes to shopping malls, movies like *Star Wars*, books like *Less Than Zero*, and the work of Foucault and Derrida ("Postmodernism" 347-48, 350). The center—and the sign—do not hold. As Jean-François Lyotard defines it, postmodernism is about "incredulity toward the metanarratives," those totalizing discourses that have structured our understanding of the world and that  are now fragmented and outmoded (*The Postmodern Condition* xxiv). Even the metanarrative of capitalism, retold each day by advertising, may be at risk. "Anything goes," Lyotard says, as  "eclecticism" becomes  the degree zero of contemporary general culture slackening into "a heterogeneity of elements" where "one listens to reggae, watches a western, eats McDonald's food for lunch and local cuisine for dinner, wears Paris perfume in Tokyo and 'retro' clothes in Hong Kong" ("Answering the Question: What Is Postmodernism?" 76). "Consensus has become an outmoded and suspect value" in this "paralogic" and play of "instabilities" (*The Postmodern Condition* 66). Even as we seek the new rules of the game, we must recognize our language  games themselves as "heteromorphous," favoring "a multiplicity of finite meta-arguments," that can be only "local," a "temporary contract" in our quest for the "parology" which "would never risk fixating in a position of minimax equilibrium" (*The Postmodern Condition* 66–67). If language's "reserve of possible utterances . . . is inexhaustible" (*The Postmodern Condition* 67), Lyotard's answer to our desire for "the realization of the fantasy to seize reality" is this: "Let us wage a war on totality; let us be witnesses to the unpresentable; let us activate the differences and save the honor of the name [reality]" ("Answering the Question: What Is Postmodernism?" 81–82).

Maybe we *can* learn from Las Vegas, that American Dream of a city where surface is all there is and where the cultural logic of late capitalism showed up early. In its jamborees of incongruous juxtaposition, its pastiche, and its privileging of advertising images—those three-dimensional, soaring shapes "before which the existing vocabulary of art history is helpless . . . Boomerang Modern, McDonald's Hamburger Parabola, Miami Beach Kidney," as Tom Wolfe remarked (qtd. in Venturi, Brown and Izenour 52)—the Las Vegas Strip is the virtual zone of postmodernism, a society of spectacle. Its discontinuities are the ones we are now learning to live with. Yet there may be in such disorder "an order we cannot see," as Henri Bergson has said (qtd. in Venturi, Brown and Izenour 52). Perhaps we are in the process of discovering it, even as what we receive through our senses overwhelms language and logic. Refusing our illusions of totality, advertising's heteroglossia trains us to inexhaustible *differance* and the apocalyptic hyperreal, setting forth the rules and procedures, the code of the postmodern world.

## NOTES

1. Indeed, the marketplace tongue of the bazaar and the street vendor, still to be heard today, may be the source of adspeak's clipped imperatives.
2.   Print does hold the gaze as TV seeks above all else to keep us watching. Interestingly, a number of TV commercials have resorted to bold black-and-white title cards full of print, which require reading—and thus a closer scrutiny of and involvement in the ad's claims on the viewer's part. This technique, as practitioners told *New York* magazine, "makes the proposition stronger," forces viewers (those who can read at least) to get involved and retain more, and allows advertisers to increase the density and impact of a commercial by

using all the effects that music and sound bites can add while the printed words are on the screen. Keeping advertising's usual authoritative voice-overs "quieter," as one ad man said, such a technique allows for better mood-enhancing aural effects such as music to tell us what to feel. The problem is that viewers *do not* sit and stare at the screen during commercials; they have trained themselves to leave the room for the refrigerator, and thus they probably miss these "quiet" print messages (Bernice Kanner, "Quiet on the Set," *New York* 14 Jan. 1991: 10–11).

Gitlin comments that the use of print subtitles to deny the claims made by "Joe Isuzu" in the 1987 series of commercials mocked "the conventions of the hard sell" and took for granted "a culture of lies" ("Postmodernism" 354).

3. Marshall Blonsky speaks of TV's need for "the empty vessel," applying the epithet to Vanna White, Ted Koppel and other media and political stars: "Make of yourself a surface so people can read in you what they want. It's today's way to govern" (comments made by Marshall Blonsky in his course "Semiotics of Advertising," The New School, New York, Fall 1988).

4. "Mass man" messages do not always work. "Just Do It," the Nike slogan, meant "one thing to the middle class [get in shape] and something else to people mired in the ghetto," setting off violent incidents involving sneakers costing more than $100 (John Leo, quoted in Warren Berger, "They Know Bo," *New York Times Magazine*, 11 Nov. 1990: 48).

5. It was D.H. Lawrence who is said to have commented, "The curious thing about art speech is that it prevaricates so terribly."

## WORKS CITED

Baudrillard, Jean. "Simulacra and Simulations." *Selected Writings.* Ed. Mark Poster. Stanford, Calif.: Stanford University Press, 1988: 166–184.

Bernstein, Basil. "A Public Language: Some Sociological Implications of a Linguistic Form." *British Journal of Sociology* 10 (1959): 311–325.

Debord, Guy. *Society of the Spectacle.* Detroit: Black & Red, 1983.

Ewen, Stuart. *All Consuming Images: The Politics of Style in Contemporary Culture.* New York: Basic Books, 1988.

Gitlin, Todd. "Hip-Deep in Postmodernism." *New York Times Book Review* 6 Nov. 1988: 1, 35–36.

————. "Postmodernism: Roots and Politics." *Cultural Politics in Contemporary America.* Ed. Ian Angus and Sut Jhally. New York: Routledge, 1989: 347–360.

Jameson, Fredric. "Postmodernism, or the Cultural Logic of Late Capitalism." *The New Left Review* 146 (July–August 1984): 53–92.

Lears, T.J. Jackson. "From Salvation to Self-Realization: Advertising and the Therapeutic Roots of Consumer Culture, 1880–1930." *The Culture of Consumption: Critical Essays in American History 1880-1980.* Ed. Richard Wightman Fox and T.J. Jackson Lears. New York: Pantheon Books, 1983: 3–38.

Lyotard, Jean-François. "Answering the Question: What Is Postmodernism?" Trans. Regis Durand. *The Postmodern Condition: A Report on Knowledge.* Trans. Geoff Bennington and Brian Massumi. Minneapolis: University of Minnesota Press, 1984: 71–82.

————. *The Postmodern Condition: A Report on Knowledge.* Trans. Geoff Bennington and Brian Massumi. Minneapolis: University of Minnesota Press, 1984.

McLuhan, Marshall, and Quentin Fiore. *The Medium Is the Massage: An Inventory of Effects,* New York: Bantam, 1967.

Meyrowitz, Joshua. *No Sense of Place: The Impact of Electronic Media on Social Behavior.* New York: Oxford University Press, 1985.

Mitchell, W.J.T. "Interview with Barbara Kruger." *Critical Inquiry* 17 (Winter 1991): 434–448.

Mueller, Claus. "Class as the Determinant of Political Communication." *American Media and Mass Culture: Left Perspectives.* Ed. Donald Lazere. Berkeley: University of California Press, 1987: 431–440.

Poster, Mark. *The Mode of Information: Poststructuralism and Social Context.* Chicago: University of Chicago Press, 1990.

Postman, Neil. *Amusing Ourselves to Death: Public Discourse in an Age of Show Business.* New York: Viking, 1985.

Pynchon, Thomas. *Vineland.* Boston: Little, Brown, 1990.

Venturi, Robert, Denise Scott Brown, and Steven Izenour. *Learning from Las Vegas: The Forgotten Symbolism of Architectural Form.* 1972. Cambridge: MIT Press, 1977.

# 2

# When Foreign Sells: Exotica in American TV Ads of the Eighties and Nineties

*Elise Salem Manganaro*

From the bejeweled Siamese cat in the commercial who languishes toward Sheba cat food to the elegant couple cruising the Caribbean by moonlight, TV ads lure with promises of foreignness. Candice Bergen's effortless French across Sprint telephone lines reinforces the ease with which we, too, can speak to faraway places. Northwest Airlines entices viewers to experience the "mystery" of the Orient, and American Express takes us there. McDonald's presents an international array of future Olympic hopefuls—toddlers that we must instinctively love—while Coca-Cola convinces us that political barriers have indeed disintegrated now, since virtually the whole world enjoys Coke. What a happy world, where nationalities mix, where Ray Charles directs a chorus of tribal Africans, Buddhist monks, Japanese crowds, and, finally, a UN delegation in an "Uh-Huh" singalong for Diet Pepsi! Surely this is harmless fun. On one level, many of these ads that adopt foreignness to pitch their sale are aesthetically pleasing, clever, humorous. Even what these ads mask, their concern for profits, is hardly reprehensible. We are all knowingly consumers in a capitalist economy and understand the necessity for commodification and competition. What is less apparent, however, is how these ads reinforce the "hierarchy, dominance, and subordination" that characterize our relations with the foreign (O'Barr 2). And perhaps even more surprising is how they expose complicated notions of Self/Other and reveal unexpected paradoxes of power and fear. My aim is to explore the multiple ways in which the Other (the foreign, the exotic) is used, and can be interpreted, in recent American TV ads. Whether the representation is overtly negative or delightfully positive, whether the Other is tropical islander or desert Arab, whether the exotic is product or backdrop, it resonates as a complex cultural product, replete with significance.

Ever since the opening of the trade routes with the Orient, the traditional exotic artifacts (silks, oils, perfumes, spices, etc.) have surfaced in Western culture as samples of Eastern luxury and "abundance." In *Fables of Abundance: A Cultural*

*History of Advertising in America*, T. J. Jackson Lears traces exoticism in early American advertising. In contrast to a Puritan ethic of frugality and simplicity, a certain strain of exoticism began to appear in the early to mid-19th century; "Oriental villas" sprang up on New England plots, divans and ottomans appeared in railroad cars, and Eastern ornaments spiced up "middle-class" homes. This luxurious tendency, writes Lears,

signified imaginative participation in a world of exotic, sensuous experience and titillating theatricality, perhaps even a faint and fitful dream of personal transformation. By the 1840's, Orientalism pervaded the exotic visions of abundance put forward by everyone from Barnum to the editors of the ladies' magazines. (63)

Soon the exotic was linked to patent medicines, most explicitly as a cure for impotence. Dr. Raphael's Cordial Invigorant of 1858 was supposedly a formula secured from an Arab bedouin king who at 109 had fathered seventy seven children (Lears 64). By the end of the century, the exotic setting became increasingly the norm for commercial images of eroticism and abundance.

## FEAR, DOMINANCE, AND THE EXOTIC

The exotic is that which is foreign or Other, not domestic. In advertising, ironically the exotic often becomes a primitive backdrop to luxury items that stand out in juxtaposition. And the many recurring exotic images in contemporary American TV ads rarely function as purely erotic or "abundant," even when they continue to lure.

An essential step in decoding the exotic begins with recognizing its essentialist mystique. Underlying seemingly positive images of the exotic are often ominous signs of fear and dominance, effectively masked by intentionally obscure representations. Robert Goldman prefaces his *Reading Ads Socially* with the following statement:

The material impact of ads lies in producing and reproducing a currency of sign values that can be joined to commodities; ideologically the sheer number of ads that we process numbs us into an acceptance of the social logic imposed by the framework of the commodity form. It is here that mystification takes place, it is here that we are encouraged to embrace reified social logic as if it were natural. (unpaged preface)

The mystification element, visible in exotic representations, encourages simplified and reductionist interpretations. TV, along with its ads, is the most powerful current example of "surface only" values, promoting a hermetically sealed discourse of association always reinforced through the TV medium. One of the most effective strategies for the ads' production of meaning is to set forth an intentionally vague and disembodied value system that is then made to somehow/seemingly represent a feature of the specific commodity on display. This tendency to "mystify" is, of course, what allows for the "exotic" to emerge at all. An abstract, but very powerful, "currency of sign values" can then dictate how the ad will be read.

American military ad campaigns, for example, illustrate a mystification at work relating to domestic/foreign relations.  The patriotic images and scenes of small-town America set against a moving rendition of "America the Beautiful" emphasize teamwork, racial harmony, "freedom," commitment, success . . . not in battle, but in college.  While focusing on military hardware, the recruit is in training for a degree in engineering, not combat.  Despite the glamour and decisive victory of the allied forces in Desert Storm, military marketing and advertising officials fear that "depictions of combat or even allusions to the reality of warfare could scare away more potential recruits than they would attract" ("The War" D1).  The military's raison d'être—offensive or defensive action against foreigners—is hence categorically denied by refusing to admit or include the foreigner, allied or foe. The American military is marketed as a series of abstractions, easily and emotionally identified with patriotic values.  Its successful advertising relies on vagueness and mystification, avoiding graphic imagery that can evoke the negative associations of war.

The same quality of vagueness is present in the "it" of American Express's "Don't leave home without it."  Not only are Americans eternally linked by some umbilical cord to their homeland, but also "it" is an undefined and intentionally fuzzy password that includes some while excluding others.  In the classic inside/outside binary, the "it" signifies the "privilege of membership."  You are a member of a community that allows you to "charge" in both an economic and a semantic sense:  You charge your purchases with the card while charging the "it" with significance.  The floating signifier "it," like the deconcretized military ad image, creates a space for the transference of fears. Instead of dwelling on the concrete and specific association of being an American abroad (whether at war or touring or on business), the undefined space becomes the locus for positive images such as freedom, friendship, and wealth.  No blown-up bodies exist in this discursive formula.

The American Express cardholder travels the globe smilingly absorbing (consuming) the beauties of foreignness while the "natives" look on, serving, guiding, accommodating.  The fact that American Express offices are blown up (in Athens on July 18, 1991—presumably a response to then-President Bush's visit) could never be acknowledged in the fantasy world of ads. The juxtaposition of the American in the international setting must always be exaggeratedly positive; anything less would trigger the latent fears that Americans have of the foreign.  We never see in these commercials any of the potentially threatening features of the so-called third world (to be discussed more fully in the section below on the Middle East).  The foreigner is the fictional Juan Valdez, who meticulously handpicks his Colombian coffee beans.  He is gracious, smiling, attentive to American tastes. The ad must work hard to distance Juan from the thought that he might smuggle cocaine in his coffee.  For how does one counter the dominant association of

Colombia with the Medellín drug cartel? So even when the ad works positively to counter negative stereotypes, it does so by mystifying its foreign subject, now visible only through an aura of goodness and benevolence.

While many companies avoided sponsoring war footage during the 1991 Gulf War, it soon became apparent that by linking their products to the fuzzy "it," the ads were sure to "hit home." A whole assemblage of ads then associated their products—from cars to sodas to fast-food chains—with patriotic good feelings as companies publicly donated goods to the troops in Saudi Arabia and used a sudden abundance of red, white and blue in their ad campaigns. America, "us," goodness, would profit from our consumerism; neither the individual profits of the company nor the mayhem being leveled at Iraq was, of course, ever marketed.

Avoiding the "ugly foreigner" by depicting the foreigner only in attractive terms not only masks the deep fears of the isolationist American, but also contributes to the narrative of expansion evident in so many of these ads. The beautification of the foreign facilitates its appropriation. Nowhere is this more apparent than in the touristic ad campaigns depicting Hawaii (once a foreign land but now conveniently the fiftieth state). Hawaii's identity has been packaged carefully to balance the foreign with the familiar; the result is a marketable commodity that lures mainlanders season after season. The intrusion of jets, helicopters, highways, hotels, golf courses, and tour buses into these fragile islands has created an artificial climate for touristic consumption. While native and local groups have been forever altered by the tourist industry, their customs have been "pristinely" preserved in the most visited (and one of the most expensive) of the touristic sites, the Polynesian Cultural Center. This Disneyland recreation of traditional huts and rural handicrafts (funded and managed by the adjacent Mormon church and community) is the most apt symbol of the domesticated foreigner, now usually a student at Brigham Young University on Oahu, reclad as the dancing Tahitian. The Polynesian as sexually uninhibited, playful and joyous, happy to please and serve, is a brilliant cover for the complex realities of these foreign islanders, though the islanders are not merely victims of American expansion; many diverse ethnic and class groups within Hawaii have participated in, and benefited from, the tourist industry, for example. The diverse, hybrid nature of these islanders, however, cannot be captured by the ad that instead constructs a mystified exotic image easily packaged on travel brochures and TV ads that continues to entice.

Most of the commercials for cruises to the Bahamas and trips to Jamaica and other Caribbean islands exhibit the same avoidance strategies. They depict only the unadulterated pink sand, the uniformed and scrubbed local schoolgirls, the skipping, smiling faces alongside the white buildings. Obviously the poverty, social unrest, and political upheaval would not go over well in an ad promoting relaxation, fantasy, and romance. It is necessary for the advertiser to insist upon the exotic mystique, the clear sense of Other in order to lure the potential customer to these foreign lands. For it is that "customer" who dominates in the end; the tourist controls the economic and discursive agency played out in the ad by appropriating the foreign and defining the terms of the relationship.

A 1981 commercial for Jamaica (well analyzed by Mark Crispin Miller) demonstrates perfectly the inherent imperialist messages of a tourist campaign. The ad depicts a variety of happy black Jamaicans beckoning the American: "Come back to gentility"; "Come back to the way things *used* to be. Make it Jamaica again, and make it your own." And while this travelogue has undergone some changes in the last few years, the same focus on a mythical, past sense of Jamaica is still strong, and the ad remains very effective. Why?

In *Boxed In: The Culture of TV*, Miller examines how this ad lures by appealing to an imagined past,

a hazy paradisiacal interlude that fell sometime between Reconstruction and the Beatles' first appearance on Ed Sullivan. We were happy, back then. Watched over by God and a few other kindly tycoons, we understood the meaning of hard work, a dollar, life itself; colored people knew their place, and nobody pushed us around. We inhabited a paradise that we can have again, the myth implies, if we just wish very hard and make no noise. (33)

This is not the Jamaica of revolutions and poverty where in recent years tourists have been attacked. No, under the conservative regime of Edward Seage, "Jamaica is once again genteel, tranquil, and romantic, a colonial idyll in need of one thing only: white masters." Here the native men play polo (evoking British imperial times), and the women offer beautiful flowers (themselves) to the camera. This is an island that has been and can once again be exploited (33–35).

The ad also promotes a plantation image, where blacks grin deferentially in clothes reminiscent of the slaves in *Gone With the Wind*, inviting the whites back not just to the Caribbean, but also to an American past where the potentially threatening black and foreigner has been fully domesticated to serve the white consumer. The urge to escape into an exotic world is reinforced by the desire to overcome its inhabitants. The inherent paradox of the American tourist, both appreciative and exploitative, suits well the paradox of the advertising medium, which promotes in order to consume.

The paradox is clear in a 1992 sequence of Northwest Airlines commercials: "To understand Asia, you have to understand its customs, its mystery, its people. You need to know what makes a good impression, or offends. For over forty years we've been learning about Asia." Sandwiched between exotic shots of the Orient are epigrammatic bits of knowledge: Thais love tulips; in Tokyo, bow whenever you see someone; in Seoul, no one drinks alone. From Tokyo to Bangkok to Singapore to Hong Kong, Northwest Airlines "can give you what no U.S. airline can: knowledge, insight and information that comes after forty years of helping people do business in Asia."

Thus, an explicitly non-threatening touristic Asia overtly masks the cut-throat competitiveness between American and Asian businesses. Northwest has not been transporting Americans to Asia for forty years merely to view the sights!

A corporate GE commercial singled out by *The Economist* also goes out of its way to mask its intention.  The ad portrays the company as a "missionary for capitalism."  The spot makes its $150 million purchase of a 50 percent stake in Tungsram (a Hungarian lighting-equipment company) look like a philanthropic investment in Eastern Europe, where "Freedom is all that matters."   While Hungarians, old and young, mingle in a scene lit up with candles and chandeliers, the voice-over gently intones: "At GE we are proud to play even a small part in helping the Hungarian people build what promises to be a truly brilliant future." Of course, the real reason for the investment (to stop Tungsram from undercutting GE in America) is never mentioned ("America's Corporate" 68).

Americans and their companies not only are comfortably situated in foreign settings, but also are needed there, welcome there.  Their reception is nothing less than heartfelt; their presence ensures—no, creates—the warmth and contentment of the  foreigners who stand graciously by their side.  The American and the foreigner, in fact, often seem to be on the same happy mission; no latent fears or hostile takeovers are overtly associated with these exotic representations.

## SELF AS EXOTICIZED OTHER

As Edward Said demonstrated in *Orientalism*, the Other is constructed and appropriated along ideological lines.  The repeated Western representations of the Oriental Other constitute a complicated, but coherent, system, internally consistent and characterized by a particular power relationship between Occident and Orient. Ironically this colonial discourse "has less to do with the Orient than it does with 'our' world" (Said 12). The hermetically sealed discourse of ads, like that of Orientalism, does not allow for the foreign subjects to truly speak. In a 1995 Isuzu ad, when the Moroccan man looks up from his coffee at the speeding Trooper Limited and asks, "Those overfenders are new, aren't they?," he is not exactly "speaking" despite the actual Arabic heard on the screen.  According to Said, it is really the voice of the colonizer (or the Isuzu sponsor) that is being heard.

In his article, "The Other Question: Difference, Discrimination, and the Discourse of Colonization," Homi Bhabha rejects what he sees as a binary division in Said's paradigm of Self and Other.  Whereas Said foregrounds the colonizer (the Self) as the sole creator of an imagined Other, Bhabha claims that one cannot even theorize the Self without constituting the Other.  There is a reciprocal interchange between colonized and colonizer, a dialogue of sorts.  Colonial power and discourse are not always possessed entirely by the colonizer, as Said would argue (Bhabha 77).  Perhaps the fact that the ministries of tourism of the vacation spots mentioned above are often themselves the sponsors of these American-made ads is a useful example of that interchange.  When the Bahamas Ministry of Tourism hires and then dismisses the Reiman Agency (Roberts 3), it underscores the increasingly transnational nature of current money flows and the increasingly reflexive nature of that constituted Other.

A striking feature of many of these ads is that despite their use of the foreign Other, they are often surprisingly familiar.  That which is "not me," the foreign, is situated in relation to the "me," the Self.  The familiar American couple is hence juxtaposed against the Great Wall of China.  The happy husband- and-wife team who have been mercifully reimbursed for their lost American Express card are so transparently American that her question on why the wall was built fittingly elicits this reply:  "It must have been a tough neighborhood."  Yes, this is something all Americans understand; the unfamiliar has been domesticated, brought "home," so to speak.  Ironically that "home" is increasingly populated by Others; those "tough neighborhoods," to the wealthy white couple, are invariably distinguished by class and race.  The rather complicated, and often paradoxical, Selves and Others created by these ads reinforce their hybrid interconnectedness.

The three young American women ("such very good friends," narrates the heavily accented Caribbean voice) on vacation in St. Thomas also have no problem replacing their lost Citibank Visa card.  As they lounge in the fun sun by the pool, they remind one of Anne Tyler's "accidental tourist," who would be happiest in the most familiar of American vacation settings, a generic hotel poolside.

In each of the ads, the "American" or an American trait is given a foreign twist. The punk teenager with his long hair, jeans, motorcycle, and loud rock music is not an expected indigenous member of the now-defunct USSR, but there he is, misunderstood like millions of American teenagers by the older generation, who then "lighten up" with Pepsi, "a generation ahead."  Pepsi, we are urged to believe, actually *generates* change.  Indeed, the global sharing of common commodities has seemingly made us all alike.  There is, Bhabha believes, a reciprocal interchange between nations of Self and Other.  The Russian "punk" is increasingly a construct that demands interpretation in conjunction with its domestic American counterpart.

"Across the world phones are ringing."  AT&T's Reach Out World commercials alternate images of foreigners and "not so" foreigners talking warmly and happily in varying accents and languages on the telephone.  Another international long-distance AT&T spot focuses on an "AT&T customer," the label for a Philippine man living in the United States who calls "home" every New Year's Eve at midnight.  His young nieces who answer the phone in the Philippines, like their uncle, not only are fluent in English, but also have no foreign accent.  As they share the sound of the fireworks, there is little doubt that the celebration is merely a Philippine version of our Fourth of July.

The Americanized foreigner, symbolically featured in a 1988 Bush/Quayle campaign ad, is ironically adapted to promote patriotic values.  As Columba Garnica Bush, the then–Vice President's daughter-in-law, tells Hispanics in Spanish that George Bush cherishes Hispanic values and traditions, she concludes, "And I believe him."  Miller's reading of this ad highlights the patriotism symbolized by the colors and the spacing of the characters.  In his red shirt, exuding Latin warmth, Bush becomes the center of this family scene.  Surrounded by children and grandchildren in red, white, and blue, Bush ends with this: "As president, I have a lotta reasons to help Hispanics everywhere—because I'll be answering to my grandkids, not just to history" (quoted in Miller, "Political Ads" 37).  Irrespective of what his record was regarding Hispanics (and other minority groups), the calculated inclusion of the foreigner in what must be the most American of families is a brilliant move.  Being Hispanic is more than just being accepted; it is advantageous.  The foreigner, a woman standing protected by the white, rich, powerful male candidate, could not be more harmless.  Indeed, here the foreigner is the American; Self and Other are one.

In a current climate of xenophobia, when Proposition 187 was passed in California in 1994, the conflation of Self and Other becomes even more ironic.  Unless the foreign is presented as exaggeratedly positive, the probable negative associations might surface to ambush the intent of the ad.

In her analysis of advertisements, Judith Williamson offers another useful perspective on the Self/Other relationship.  People, she concludes, become

signified by, and then summarized by, things. . . . This should make clear the very real material basis and substructure of the images that are valued and exchanged in society. . . We re-create ourselves every day, in accordance with an ideology based on property—where we are defined by our relationship to things, possessions, rather than to each other.  (179)

Since the exotic Other has been objectified and essentialized, it is an example of the "material" that helps define the American Self.  The American is often seen in conjunction with, in juxtaposition to, or in possession of the foreign.  At times the foreign, as we saw in the Bush/Quayle campaign ad, becomes the domestic.  The roles are conflated, even reversed, in a 1992 ad shown on British TV that objectifies nothing less than an entire nation.  Then-President Bush, hands in his pockets, walks gingerly across a golf course, trying to sell America: "America's a land of contrast, from rolling green fields, to sandy white beaches, to red hot Dixieland jazz" (Lippert 24).  Directed to foreigners, the ad presents America as Other, a tourists' haven, where all possible unpleasantries have been smoothed over by a green, rolling terrain and a reassuring salesman.  The product is essentialized into a positive, digestible entity to be consumed.  In the end, Americans are also foreigners—not only outside U.S. borders, but also to themselves.  One can be exoticized by makeup, travel, food, or attire; the new image is attractive, desirable.  The old, unadulterated image is often repellent, calling out for a face-lift.  Consider the Before and After photos of those women's faces that stare out at us from glossy magazine pages.  Are they any different from the transformations that occur on TV commercials when the American tourist is viewed swirling her skirts to a foreign beat, having left her mundane life behind in Nowhere, Idaho?  And when the Self, as Bhabha argues, is constructed always in conjunction with the Other, it is no wonder that representations of the foreign end up revealing much about the domestic.

## THE TROUBLING MIDDLE EASTERN EXOTIC

While early American advertising adopted exotic (primarily "Middle Eastern" driven) images to suggest "abundance," and while the exotic East was once the site of an imagined luxury, it now primarily serves as a contrasting primitive backdrop to Western luxury items. Three 1995 television ads with Arab/Islamic settings demonstrate this new paradigm at work:

In what is supposed to be a traditional Arab marketplace, bustling with ancient wares and traditional merchandise, two men discuss, in Arabic, new IBM services.

A couple lost in the desert are directed by a young Arab boy calling "ATM, ATM" to a primitive-looking village that miraculously among the traditional artifacts displays a modern automatic teller machine.

During the 1995 Super Bowl, Isuzu released its new ad for the Trooper Limited; filmed in Morocco, the ad (Agency: Goodby, Silverstein and Partners) uses English subtitles on an Arabic script. Again, in a traditional Arab/Muslim setting the "natives" go about their business in the town bazaar: the men sipping coffee or shaving amongst the carpets for sale, the women preparing wool (presumably for the carpets), and the boys playing soccer on a makeshift sandy field. Against a backdrop of a caravan of camels and a muezzin's call to prayer, a Trooper Limited flashes by. The Arabs, now used to this "annual marathon" through North Africa, look up from their indigenous activities to comment perceptively and knowingly about this technological wonder. For example, a woman in traditional garb laboring over the wool that she has just draped across a line comments, "Hey, they tweaked the suspension." Another woman adds, "Check it out, dual airbags." The main impact of the ad lies, of course, in its ludicrous juxtapositions: the super-sophisticated product of Western technology cutting a swath across a culture that seems frozen in time and the illiterate Muslim woman able to discern technical features of a vehicle she could never possess.

IBM, ATM, and Isuzu artifacts are the new luxury items that are set to best advantage against a depleted setting. The exotic East is no longer abundant, but it can still be useful in marketing products in the West.

Another feature of the mentioned ads is that they are all set in the Arab/Islamic world. This fact would not ordinarily have great significance, except that American TV ads have in the past generally steered away from depiction of Arab or Muslim images. (Certain print ads in the seventies and eighties, however, intentionally presented the feared Arab/Muslim as the evil oil-monger; the message, of course, was to shift blame for higher oil prices). If, as Roland Marchand argues, "Advertisers sought only those notes that would evoke a positive resonance" (xix), it would make absolute sense to avoid any image of an Arab (read terrorist) or a Muslim (read fundamentalist) that might trigger fears associated with these negative stereotypes. The reason why we are now seeing Arabs as promoters, by association, of these products can perhaps be explained in part by the emergence of a new political order in the Middle East.

In his study of print ads, *Culture and the Ad: Exploring Otherness in the World of Advertising*, William O'Barr explicitly foregrounds the political in his analysis. His main argument is as follows:

The representations of foreigners and other categories of outsiders who appear in advertisements provide paradigms for relations between members of advertising's intended audience and those defined as outside it. These paradigms constitute an ideological guide for relations between the self and others, between us and them. The most frequently depicted qualities of such relationships are hierarchy, dominance, and subordination. (2)

The American victory in Desert Storm not only ensured a powerful U.S. military presence in the Gulf states, but also opened up new markets in the region. With virtually no credible surviving counterbalance to U.S. influence in the Gulf, the balance of power shifted dramatically, allowing for new constructs of the Arab. With Arabs split, however, over defending or destroying Saddam Hussein, representations of the Arab would still have to be very carefully negotiated. It is no surprise, then, that the images of Arabs now visible on TV evoke Morocco and the Gulf, both relatively "friendly" military regions, and not Syria and Egypt, although the latter two states also opposed Iraq's invasion of Kuwait. Syria is still considered a "terrorist" nation, and Egypt is too visible as a site for anti-Western militant Islamic fundamentalism. But the "moderate" Arab states offer useful new markets , which since the Gulf War have been inundated by American businesses leading in the reconstruction of Kuwait. The allegiances, therefore, between Arab nations and the Unites States during that war, coupled by closer economic relations, have resulted in an altered climate of U.S./Arab relations. Given the unbalanced nature of the relation, it is still characterized by O'Barr's "hierarchy, dominance, and subordination," but the terms of the debate have changed. The two groups can now be pitched as military and economic partners, opening up a new arena for *seemingly* positive representations such as those we have seen in recent TV ads.

A sure clue that the climate was altered was visible in the 1995 Doritos Super Bowl half time show. While Patti LaBelle and Tony Bennett sang to an oriental-sounding tune, "within our desert caravan," and an Indiana Jones–like rescue was taking place on stage, the main focus was on the hundreds of dancers/performers clad in a mishmash of "foreign" attires. The bodies wore Aztec, Polynesian, African, Native American, and, significantly, Islamic dress. Costumes were mixed and matched: a Turkish pantaloon, a cavewoman holster top, a Native American headdress, a veil. The busy backdrop featured African cauldrons with dancing savages, slithering snakes within an Arab bazaar, belly dancers and acrobats, gaudy Las Vegas dancers, sinister foreign-looking criminals (who steal the trophy that will be rescued by the Indiana Jones figure), all in a dizzying mosaic of movement and color that signified . . . what? Excess, appropriation, globalization, spectacle? As the act reached its climax, the dancers whirled about, and the camera focused on those in Islamic dress, who then proceeded to remove their scarves and head covers and wave them in a gesture of liberation.

An estimated 120 million people watched all or part of this Super Bowl XXIX game, in which the foreign is brought in to perform, to sell, to contrast, to exoticize, and to frighten.  The foreign is turned into an identifiable object to be altered, improved, replaced.  It is made to adorn a chorus line or to espouse a political agenda.  The dancers in Islamic dress, made to appear very much like Iranian pro-Khomeini supporters, obviously reject what is perceived to be an oppressive aspect of their religion.  The "desert caravan" of the main song's refrain is presented much like Disney's world of *Aladdin*, a generic exotic locale reminiscent of pre-bombed Baghdad, Hollywood Casablanca, dangerous Kabul, populated by a mysterious troupe of peoples, combining features from Morocco to India along the Islamic belt that sweeps across north Africa and southern Asia.

In light of the April 19, 1995, terrorist bombing in Oklahoma City, which was immediately blamed on Arabs and Muslims who were then arrested, targeted, and falsely accused, it is obvious that the entire Middle East is still much maligned and stereotyped in American culture.  Despite more visible representations of Arabs and Muslims on TV, a climate of fear and distrust (fueled by various political interest groups) still characterizes the relation between the American Self and the Middle Eastern Other.

In 1994, the Council on American-Islamic Relations (CAIR) was formed to present an "Islamic perspective on issues of importance to the American public."  Among the council's missions is monitoring the media, and its members have already been successful in alerting the public to "offensive" TV ads and having them altered or removed.  In March 1995, the Phoenix-based Doubletree Hotel Corporation agreed to alter TV ads that depicted hotel employees dressed in "Arabian" clothing "praying" to guests in the same way that Muslims pray to God.  In December 1994, Anheuser-Busch apologized to the Muslim community for use of an Islamic religious phrase (from the Koran) printed on the tank-top of a model in a beer commercial (CAIR Press Release).

Removal of the most blatantly insulting ads is a good thing, but more subtle representations are left intact.  In the IBM commercial featuring two young Arab men conversing about how to get a company on-line, it is worth noting that while one of the Arabs is enquiring about how to get the best technology, the other Arab (and not a Westerner) provides him with the necessary information: Contact IBM.  Both men are on e-mail, they both have a facility with computers, and they are successful modern businessmen.  Their location in an antiquated Arab souk, however, reinforces the amazing expanse of an American company that can reach the furthest corners of the globe.  And here the depoliticized "natives" are receptive to change, unconcerned by the turmoils of class, corruption, or postcolonial confusion.

In ads encouraging travel to foreign climes, the tourist is made to feel perfectly comfortable and unthreatened.  The indigenous peoples are exaggeratedly docile and subservient; any suggestions to the contrary would alarm viewers who are already wary of growing anti-American sentiment abroad.  When the foreign is reduced to an image to be appropriated and used in conjunction with a product (like perfume or cat food) that has nothing to do with the advertised item, then "advertising is little concerned with the accuracy of the images it constructs" (O'Barr 12). It is in these ads that older notions of exoticism as practiced in early American advertising surface: The foreign promises romance, mystique, escape, abundance.

## THE EXOTIC IN A GLOBAL ECONOMY

Most of the ads discussed up until this point present a seemingly positive representation of the exotic Other, but some ads are overtly negative. In this xenophobic and highly competitive economic culture, America's questionable performance at home has generated genuine fear and insecurity most clearly seen in car commercials. A 1990 ad for Pontiac dealers in the New York metropolitan area ominously predicts that if Americans keep buying Japanese cars, then the yearly ritual of visiting Rockefeller Center will be transformed into seeing "the big Christmas tree at Hirohito Center." "Go on," the announcer challenges, "keep buying Japanese cars." Another Oldsmobile dealer's spot for the Cutlass Sierra compares the average (or superior) height of American men with that of Japanese men and concludes, "That's why our car is built for our size families, not theirs." Other advertisers "feature ominous references to the late Emperor Hirohito, photographs of Samurai warriors, [and] exaggerated accents" (Rothenberg A1). If in April 1995 a U.S. senator (D'Amato) would take the risk on the airwaves and mimic the accent of a judge (Ito) of Japanese origin, we know that a sentiment of prejudice does exist in this society (despite the outrage that followed). The ads mentioned above purposefully accentuate the distinction between "them" and "us."

Another spot for Chrysler's luxury car LeBaron opens with a shot of the Japanese yen. As soft music plays, the yen burns, and the words "Today, the average price of a Japanese luxury car is $31,777" appear on the screen. Then a Deutsche mark appears and also burns: "The average price of a German luxury car is $52,525." The voice-over then concludes: "Introducing luxury for people who don't have money to burn." LeBaron sells for less than $14,000. While some of these commercials (especially those by local dealers) have supposedly embarrassed the GM and Chrysler companies, the corporate ads are hardly less xenophobic. Chrysler's then-chairman, Lee A. Iacocca, appears before the public in his ads admitting the quality of the imports: "The competition is good, We have to be better." He then focuses on the "stuff America was made of: quality, hard work, commitment." Without mentioning Japan by name, a patriotic American theme is clearly projected. A commercial for Dodge does not focus on quality or the specific car product at all; instead, the company is selling America. The theme, "Our own precious freedom, We celebrate America," is followed by images of Moscow and then, even more threatening, Beijing. The specter of Tiananmen Square (where democracy and freedom were so memorably crushed) is then juxtaposed with the Statue of Liberty: Liberty, freedom, democracy vs. Communist dictatorships. Dodge advertisers surmised that the powerful American abstractions (the undefined "it"), even at the expense of specific foreign markets, would outweigh the unlikely possibility of opening car dealerships in Beijing soon.

But even if Dodge were to test the Chinese market, it would (like so many transnational corporations) hire a global advertising agency that would ensure appropriate strategies for marketing in different cultures.   McCann-Erikson Worldwide is just such an agency, generating huge profits from its overseas ads in over fifty countries (O'Leary 42).  Its strategies differ depending on client and culture.  For Coca-Cola, the McCann-Erikson team of New York-based writers creates ads that can be used in many different countries:

By relying on voice-over soundtracks, the advertisers make substitutions of language a relatively easy matter.   Because the actors look neither too Scandinavian nor too Mediterranean, they can be imagined to be nationals of many different countries whose populations have European heritage. (O'Barr 199)

For these ads, the message is that we are all basically the same.  Despite surface differences, we all share in a common universality captured by our appreciation of Coke.  O'Barr continues:

Perhaps one of the consequences of the globalization of markets, the increase in the availability of the same goods and services around the world, and the emergence of generic consumers who are portrayed as sharing common desires will be a decrease in the otherness of foreigners.  (200)

If the Russian who drinks Pepsi seems familiarly "punk," does that mean he is less foreign?  All across the so-called third world, children don Nike tee-shirts, crave McDonald's, and recognize Michael Jackson.  Are differences across cultures obliterated or simply masked by these Western commodities?  I would argue that the "otherness" of foreigners as it is presented in TV ads has always been a Western construct bearing only a superficial resemblance to a genuine quality inherently attached to the foreign object per se. The producer of the TV image can choose to emphasize or deemphasize the foreign element depending on need.

Another agency, YAR Communications, with billings close to $120 million and employees who speak over thirty languages, believes that "people in any market will respond best to communications from advertisers with cultural authenticity—an authenticity that goes beyond language to encompass core values and traditions" (Sloan D16).  In opposition to the universal message approach of Coca-Cola, YAR's AT&T ads in Poland, for example, are specifically designed to appeal to the love for sentimentality and poetry of the Polish people.  This "more intimate approach to global advertising" (D16) somehow validates and authenticates cultural distinctions.

In this global economy, production and labor are often centered in the once "exotic" climes, while consumption is still centered at home.  Foreign products are now increasingly competing with domestic goods.  American companies have subsidiary plants abroad, and single products are routinely assembled by workers in various countries.   While the obvious message of so many of the car ads mentioned earlier is to Buy American in order to save the U.S. economy, the ironic reality is that it is not at all clear what *is* American any more.  With parts and labor crossing all national boundaries in search of higher profitability, the composite car product is a variation on the postmodern pastiche.  The Dodge Stealth made by Mitsubishi and sold in the United States, the Honda made in Ohio, and the Ford mini-van also produced in Ohio in a joint venture with Nissan are all examples of the cross-fertilization between the competitors turned collaborators.   While Chrysler owns nearly 11 percent of the Mitsubishi Motors Corporation, and GM owns a stake in Isuzu Motors, the Ford Motor Company uses its Japanese partner, Mazda Motor, to make cars for sale to Japanese consumers (Sanger A1, A10).  That the product slips between our semantic labels creates the rather humorous situation of advertising against the product.  By bashing the Japanese product, the American may also stand to lose.  In this multinational corporate world, patriotic slogans often take on a skewed meaning.  The increasingly hybrid nature of our cultures (of our Selves and our Others) is a testimony to this global market phenomenon.

One of the offshoots of this global economy is the emergence of multicultural marketing institutionalized in giant ad agencies.  The mentality of these agencies best captures the current status of the domestic/foreign equation.  Bruce Nelson, executive vice president/director of worldwide accounts at McCann-Erikson, explains:

McCann is a culture of cooperation and coordination.  We've become a learning organization.  We view the whole world as a giant marketing laboratory where we're dealing with clients of varying degrees, with centralized and decentralized organizations.  We're constantly learning from this experience. Everything is a test market for us. (Quoted in O'Leary 44)

With Other (and Self), product, and culture all subject to test-marketing, the ad is hardly innocent.  It is in the final analysis an essential tool in the competitive world of marketing.

One of the more interesting examples of that "global" competitiveness is visible (behind the scenes) in the competing ads for the Olympic events.  The same spirit of wholesome fun and healthy competition that characterizes the Games is overtly reflected in some of the TV ads that help bring the Games to our homes.  Coca-Cola, during the 1992 Winter Olympic Games in Albertville, France, aired sixty-second spots featuring different groups of foreigners (from Thai monks to African hut dwellers) enjoying the Games (and a Coke).  Another ad selectively focuses on a handsome young Lithuanian athlete, now free to compete for his new nation.  In his accented English, he contemplates new found freedom, linked perfectly to the newly discovered drink in the unmistakable red can.  Coke supports these athletes as it supports the Games and the Olympic spirit.  The cut-throat competition between Coca-Cola and Pepsi (which opted for Super Bowl, rather than Olympic

Games, sponsorship) is perhaps more characteristic of some of the competing athletes. Rarely, however, is the consumer invited behind the scenes to share in the scheming and gloating; the ad always attempts to mask the passionately "uncivilized" forces that propel it.

The surprisingly public 1992 battle between two corporate competitors reveals the far side of Olympic sponsorship. Visa International paid $20 million to the International Olympic Committee to be the official credit card of the 1992 Games in Albertville, France, and Barcelona, Spain. One of their ads claimed, "The Olympics don't take American Express." American Express responded with an "ambush marketing" strategy, claiming that the Visa ads were misleading, since they implied that people going to the Olympics could not use their American Express cards. As American Express created seven new customer-service centers in the French Alps, it released a series of Olympic-related ads for both TV and print media. In a *New York Times* article, Stuart Elliott writes:

The word Olympics and the five-ringed Olympic symbol were noticeably absent, since Visa had paid for the rights to use them. Instead, the advertising addressed cardholders who intend to visit the "French Alps for all the winter fun and games" and "to support our teams." (Elliott D1)

Again, the issue of semantics and delicate wording (note that the "g" in the "games" of the American Express ad is lower case) can mean the difference between litigation and profit. And while the two American giants continued to accuse each other of foul play, the international competition at the Games proceeded. Under the guise of cooperation, the foreign arena becomes yet another locus for corporate warfare.

The multifaceted use of the foreign in American TV ads exposes a network of hidden meanings and intentions. While the exotic can be used for both attracting and repelling the consumer, it also becomes a mask for ideological ventures such as appropriation, subjugation, and dominance. The untroubling images of foreignness both undermine and underscore the fears associated with the Other and promote the stereotypes that prevent significant communication between and across cultural boundaries. The economic component of the foreign "inclusion" translates into the objectification of the foreign and its reduction into a commodity useful only in its exchange value. As multi- and transnational corporations tighten their grip on world economies, the perception of the foreign as exotic "pawn" clarifies as well notions of Self.

As a focused example of the exotic, the representations of Arabs and Muslims suggest that ads serve a political as well as an economic agenda: Lucrative Arab markets now exist because of the Gulf War. While these ads seem to make positive associations between the Middle Easterner and the product, they reinforce paradigms of dominance and are often insulting. The overstated passive and friendly Arab is only masking what the Arab can so quickly be transformed into: the terrorist striking at the heartland of America. The fears linked to this Other become part of the constructed exotic, who then displays traits of the creator, the Self.

At the very least, TV ads are revelatory: They reflect back on the Self, on the culture that produces them. By focusing on how these ads refer and respond to the exotic and the foreign, we can better understand ourselves and our Others. The reflexive dimension of this analysis highlights how advertising strategy is socially constructed, how chosen symbols reverberate with significance, how paradox determines meaning. Reinforcing relations of dominance, the ambivalent exotic also lures viewers to transform, to travel, to experience romance and adventure. Yet this contradiction, among others, is amazingly flattened by the TV screen, which best evokes a postmodern depthlessness in favor of a decorative and lucrative exhilaration. For in the end, the exotic Others are neither hybrid, nor complex, nor real. They serve as malleable images of juxtaposition to equally uncomplicated images of Self.

## WORKS CITED

"America's Corporate Flag-Waving Rednecks Redux." *The Economist* (21–27 July, 1990): 68+.

Bhabha, Homi K. "The Other Question: Difference, Discrimination, and the Discourse of Colonization." *Out There: Marginalization and Contemporary Cultures*. Ed. Russell Ferguson et al. Cambridge, Mass.: MIT Press, 1990: 71–87.

CAIR (Council on American-Islamic Relations) Press Release. "DoubleTree Hotel Chain Alters TV Ads Deemed Offensive to Muslims." 16 Mar. 1995.

Elliott, Stuart. "Companies Go for the Gold, Using Ambush Marketing." *New York Times* 3 Feb. 1992: D1+.

Goldman, Robert. *Reading Ads Socially*. London: Routledge, 1992.

Hutcheon, Linda. *The Politics of Postmodernism*. London: Routledge, 1989.

Jameson, Fredric. "Postmodernism and Consumer Society." *Amerika Studien* (1984): 55–73.

Lears, T. J. Jackson. *Fables of Abundance: A Cultural History of Advertising in America*. New York: Basic Books, 1994.

Lippert, Barbara. "That Vision Thing: President Bush Implores Foreigners to See a Cut-Rate USA." *Adweek* 13 Jan. 1992: 24.

Marchand, Roland. *Advertising the American Dream: Making Way for Modernity, 1920–1940*. Berkeley: University of California Press, 1985.

Miller, Mark Crispin. *Boxed In: The Culture of TV*. Evanston, Ill.: Northwestern University Press, 1988.

———. "Political Ads: Decoding Hidden Messages." *Columbia Journalism Review* (Jan./Feb. 1992): 36–39.

O'Barr, William. *Culture and the Ad: Exploring Otherness in the World of Advertising*. Boulder, Colo.: Westview Press, 1994.

O'Leary, Noreen. "Worldwide Creative: McCann-Erikson: A Blueprint for Campaigns that Travel Around the World." *Adweek* 31 Oct. 1994: 42–45.

Roberts, Elizabeth. "Bahamas Goes Back in Play." *Adweek* 21 1994: 3.

Rothenberg, Randall. "U.S. Ads Increasingly Attack Japanese and Their Culture." *New York Times* 11 July 1990: A1+.

Said, Edward. *Orientalism*. New York: Vintage Books, 1978.

Sanger, David. "Detroit Leaning on Japan, in Both Senses." *New York Times* 27 Feb. 1992: A1+.

Sloan, Leonard. "Realizing That the World Does Not Sing in Perfect Harmony," YAR Marches to Each Culture's Drum." *New York Times* 17 Feb. 1995: D16.

"The War in Military Ads? What War?" *New York Times* 8 Mar. 1991: D1+.

Williamson, Judith. *Decoding Advertisements: Ideology and Meaning in Advertising*. London: Marion Boyars, 1978.

# 3

# Some Versions of the Pastoral: Myth in Advertising; Advertising as Myth

*Martin Green*

> If your heart is here, the rest of you may stay, too.
> —Advertisement for the Princeville Resort, Kauai, Hawaii
>
> What wond'rous Life in this I lead!
> —Andrew Marvell, "The Garden"

A lone couple appear in semi-silhouette—the woman seated under a bamboo umbrella, the man standing to her right gazing out, both sheltered by huge palms that dwarf them. The sky is immense—further dwarfing the human figures in the foreground. The light is purple, yellow, flecked with gray clouds. This ad, part of a two-page display that appeared in the *New York Times Magazine* in early 1992, is a visual evocation of paradise, reinforced by copy that promises that "nature's abundance is everywhere." The bold headline, spare in the manner of contemporary copywriting, proclaims: "Magnificent. By Nature." The companion ad echoes this declaration: "Inspired. By Nature." And the second ad more explicitly compares the Princeville Resort in Hawaii, the subject of these ads, to "Eden."

That an ad for a vacation resort—complete with forty-five-hole golf course and "every water sport known to man"—consciously calls up one of humanity's oldest myths—the myth of paradise—is not completely surprising. In fact, it has become almost a cliché of vacation advertising, as a glance through a travel magazine confirms. The *New York Times' Sophisticated Traveler,* a supplement to its Sunday magazine, usually provides page after page of advertising photos of unspoiled beaches, mountain resorts, foreign villages, and retirement communities in which life is lived close to nature, in simple harmony with sun, water, and flora and fauna. Vacations, especially in foreign climes, are meant to take us away from the mundane and rejuvenate us by putting us back in touch with something primitive, remote, exotic. Ads for foreign scenes are often constructed on a paradoxical blend of the familiar and the Other, weaving a nostalgic imagery of a lost past recuperable in the present.

## THE MYTH OF THE PASTORAL: PARADISE LOST

The Edenic myth evoked in the Princeville ads connects to an equally long-standing impulse in western civilization—the pastoral. Northrop Frye identified the pastoral impulse as one of our culture's shaping myths, one of our fundamental archetypes. Both biblical and classical in origin, this archetype looks back to Eden or to a lost Golden Age as the image of the idealized world from which humanity fell. Ever since Adam and Eve (the couple in the ad?) were cast out of paradise, humankind has been longing to return there. Not being able to do so, we console ourselves with simulacra—representations, approximations—of it. In classical antiquity, the Theocritan-Vergilian pastoral provided the simulacrum in the kingdom of Arcadia, in which male and female shepherds embodied an idealized image of humanity close to, if not actually in, an unfallen state. As literary historian Bruno Snell put it: "The dream of the golden age is as old as man's thinking about the course of the world, no matter whether it springs from a sense of bewilderment, in which case it is remembered as a paradise at the beginning of time, or whether it embodies the ideals of man's positive striving, projected into the end of history" (294–95).

The pastoral myth is founded on an identification of humanity and nature—a harmony and oneness between the natural and the human. In the pastoral world, humanity is in nature and part of nature; there is no division between what humanity constructs and what nature creates. As Frye puts it, the mood of the pastoral is idyllic (46). It is also radically opposed to notions of civilization; as Frye suggests, the pastoral idyll as literary form represents escape from the confines of society, whose artificial norms and structures separate humanity from the freedom of nature. Nature defines the ideal. The development of a highly mechanized and increasingly urbanized civilization enhances the sense of split between the human world in nature and the world of nature, which makes the pastoral impulse stronger as civilization's dark satanic mills extend themselves over the landscape. Freed from, but still rooted in, classical and biblical tropes, the nineteenth-century Romantics attempted to return to the origin of being in Eden or, failing that quest, to seek its image in the unspoiled places of the world or at least to continue to use it as the standard against which civilization is judged.

America has been strongly marked by the pastoral ideal. In its earliest manifestation to European colonizers, the vast continent of America appeared to be a new Eden, a virgin land, where the ripeness of nature provided a bounty for the taking or a field on which a new civilization could be erected free of the sins of European society. Throughout our history, the land, the frontier, the wilderness took on an "immense moral significance," as one recent scholar of the pastoral in American life has put it: "Here was a new continent offering an opportunity, never before equaled, to begin life anew by returning to a simpler rural past" (Machor 4). As writers from D.H. Lawrence to Leslie Fiedler have argued, the basic impulse in much of American culture has been the rejection of "civilization" by an escape to the wilderness, to the rural and remote. The pastoral ideal was enshrined in the early days of the American republic by the Jeffersonian republican ideal of America as a society of rural yeomen living close to the soil.  Many nineteenth-century movements for political and social reform took their impulse from variations of the pastoral ideal—Thoreauvian simplicity, vegetarianism—as did, ironically, the ideology of southern slave society.  The quest for the simple life, the life unsullied by the complications of progressive society, remained a powerful yearning, infusing life and art, politics and popular culture, as David Shi has recounted.

## ADVERTISING, MODERNITY, THE MACHINE, AND THE PASTORAL

But in the modern age, the quest for the pastoral is complicated by the virtual triumph of the machine civilization that the pastoral opposes.  In the age of the machine, it becomes more difficult to find an area untouched by civilization.  As Judith Williamson argues in her *tour de force* structuralist analysis of modern advertising, the power of modern, technologically based civilization rests in its ability to define the terms of life so that the constructed world of modern life becomes the norm, becomes "natural."  Thus, the terms of the opposition between nature and culture in the pastoral archetype, in which nature is the privileged term, are reversed.  Culture becomes nature, and nature becomes subsumed in culture; with this reversal, the pastoral ideal becomes accessible only through the ministrations of culture.

Advertising grew up contemporaneously with the triumph of the machine and the emergence of modernism in the arts.  Although often opposed to the depradations of the industrial age and pastoralist in sympathy, the classical modernists' attempt to make over all the arts on a new basis often implicated them in the technologically based culture founded on the power of the machine they feared.  "Make It New," Ezra Pound's rallying cry, the prevailing credo of artistic modernism, was also that of  Henry Ford and the host of anonymous advertising professionals (or those who hoped to turn advertising from a trade into a profession).  This credo was their call to a new sense of advertising's role.  As Roland Marchand has so ably recounted, with the industrial world poised to offer up a host of new products to a growing consumer population, the world was on the verge of change, and the ad men (they were then mostly men) were its heralds, seeing themselves as apostles of modernity.  The objects of their appeals, the nascent consumers, needed to be transformed along with the transformation of the economy and industry.  Consuming was a novel experience for most people of modest means.  But the buying of products suffused with newness was both a prime symbol of transformation and a mark of modernity.  The producers of advertising had to develop appeals that would convert a traditional society into one based on new principles.

Marchand perceives several strategies structuring early advertising, what he calls the "Great Parables."  Some of these parables (the Parable of the First

Impression; the Parable of the Democracy of Goods) tapped into the fears and insecurities of a population ill at ease with its sense of identity in an age of dislocation and transformation, longing for social acceptance and doing the "right thing," which the products, of course, would allow them to do. One of these parables, which Marchand calls the Parable of Civilization Redeemed, works in a contrary way to the others, appropriating the myths and images of traditional culture, especially the pastoral. While most advertising celebrated the superiority of modernity and technology, ads that were structured on the Parable of Civilization Redeemed saw a darker side to the gifts of modern civilization. Along with the benefits of modern technology came a host of modern ills: nervousness, irregularity, physical softness, and ironically the drudgery of the very work that made the benefits of modernity possible. The triumph of civilization, the Parable implied, was at the expense of nature. As an ad for Squibb pharmaceuticals maintained, "man outwitted nature—and *lost!*" (Marchand 223). The overrefinement of food to meet new, modern standards of taste had robbed food of its natural nutrients, an argument used by nineteenth-century diet reformers like Sylvester Graham, inventor of the Graham cracker (Green). Other advertisers cautioned about the dangers of a body out of synchronization with natural rhythms, the result of the frenetic pace of modern life and the imbalances in diet. The cure for these ills was to reclaim the "natural" in life, something the ads equated with a "healthful, hard-working past" (Marchand 224). The ads, Marchand writes, "not only contrasted a healthful, hard-working past with an indolent, potentially degenerate present; [they] also seemed, on occasion, to elevate ancient or `natural' men over civilized moderns" (224). But the ads also reversed their overt message. The cure for modernity's ills lay *not* in a return to the past, but in a further application of modernity in the guise of the products the ads touted. Taking Squibb vitamins or eating bran cereal or chewing Dentyne gum was the answer to civilization's problems; these products restored regularity, provided nutrients, or gave the mouth natural exercise equivalent to an Eskimo's chewing whale blubber. This Parable structure is still resonant in contemporary advertising, as the Princeville Resort ads suggest.

The ads for the Princeville Resort and others evoke paradise in much the way the Parable of Civilization Redeemed did in the twenties and fit into Williamson's category of ads that appear to establish nature, the primitive, the Edenic ground of being, as the standard by which things are to be valued, but in fact evoke more insistently the human-made world. In the Princeville ads, it is the world of "ultra-luxury" hotels, with its concert music, overstuffed furniture, and "the invigorating lifestyle" the resort provides or makes possible, that is the co-equal of nature; in fact, it is culture, or, more precisely, the artifacts of a material civilization (golf courses, water sports), that sets the standard of value. This is reinforced by the second ad of the two-page series, which is photographed indoors. Two couples are shown: To the right, a woman is seated gazing out of a floor-to-ceiling picture window with her companion to her left gazing at her; to the left, a man sits at a grand piano while his companion plays a flute. The room is lush with tropical flowers and plush furniture covered in floral fabric. The colors echo the outdoor scene: purple and yellow. Beyond the window is water and a cliff and the cloud-flecked sky. Nature in Kauai, Hawaii, has been taken over by the taming hand of the ITT-Sheraton chain (the builders of Princeville). Wild, untamed nature—evoked in the first ad by towering palms and immense sky—has been domesticated in the second ad, put behind or outside a picture window; the blooms of paradise have been put into pots.[1]

## THE MACHINE IN THE GARDEN

This pattern of nature encompassed by the products of industrial culture is apparent in   advertising for the most technological of modern products: the automobile. In recent years, car ads, when they are not shrieking the benefits of low lease prices, evoke a curiously modern version of the pastoral.

In a Toyota ad of a few years ago (created by Saatchi and Saatchi), the natural scene is magnificent: In the background a waterfall cascades over massive rocks (Figure 1). In the foreground, huge trees frame the cliff from which the water spills. Dwarfed by the power of nature, a couple (a modern Adam and Eve in hiking gear) can be seen at the extreme edge of the photo, gazing at the turbulent flow of water amid the majesty of the rocks. The setting is the San Juan Mountains in Colorado. This is not only an earthly paradise; it is, as the copy proclaims, also a "bit of heaven." Like the Princeville ads, this ad evokes unspoiled nature, extolls the value of escape from civilization back to a pristine, unspoiled wilderness. And like the Princeville ads, it also asserts the power of modern technology over nature. For this bit of paradise (a scant twenty miles from Purgatory, Colorado) is made accessible, is reclaimed for human habitation—or at least temporary residence—by a Toyota 4Runner, a "muscular" off-road vehicle with 3.0 liter V6 engine. The gleaming red vehicle—shot from a low angle—dominates the foreground, making even the magnificent waterfall seem small. This prime embodiment of technical civilization stands triumphant over nature, containing within its "luxury interior" another mark of that civilization, a compact disc player so that the couple's journey can be accompanied by the right mood music.

A TV ad of the same year for the Mitsubishi Montero, a luxury off-road, all-purpose vehicle similar to the Toyota 4Runner (and descending from the most work-a-day of vehicles, the Jeep, which in its modern incarnation is usually depicted in ads set against the splendors of the Rockies), evokes a similar contrast of civilization and nature. The Montero is seen in the distance serenely undulating over rolling green hills across which meanders a herd of sheep. In the foreground are thatched-roofed houses, suggesting the English countryside. If paradise is too far removed in myth, its simulacrum is the unspoiled world of the nearer agricultural past. (The evocation of Englishness also diverts attention from the fact that this is a Japanese vehicle: a double bonus at the time when concerns over the

The Toyota 4Runner is photographed from a low angle to dominate the foreground and stand triumphant over nature, asserting the power of modern technology. In the distance, a modern Adam and Eve in hiking gear are pictured enjoying "this bit of heaven." Reprinted by permission of Toyota Motor Sales.

threat of Japanese industrial and financial domination of the United States were near fever pitch.)

These were but two early ads for products that have since become dominant in the auto industry.  The off-road vehicle with its aggressive engine, fat tires, and masculine aura has become the vehicle of choice not only for outdoor types but for urbanites seeking both security from the threats of modern city life and escape from that urban nightmare.  A more recent series of TV ads for Isuzu's version of this vehicle—the Trooper—depict drivers, almost always men, fleeing the restraints of modern life into the wilds of nature.  And in this series, the escape is particularly aggressive as the driver slams his vehicle through mud and rivers, thus figuring the triumph of the technological over the natural.  But at the same time, the impulse of the escape is to reclaim the world of childhood freedom, when one guiltlessly played in mud puddles, a version of the pastoral in William Empson's famous formulation.

Some car ads evoke pastoral nature even when nature is not directly depicted.  The pastoral "natural" world here is embodied in the product itself, thus completing the total appropriation of nature by technologically based culture.  In a 1990 ad for the luxury Lexus LS400, the main photograph, spread over two pages in *The New Yorker,* is of the interior of the vehicle, with its seats of rich leather.  The copy sets up a contrast between the pressure-filled world of the business executive—"ringing telephones, mounting pressures and impending deadlines"—from which escape is sought and the hermetically sealed, precision-engineered interior of the automobile that provides that refuge.  The ad appeals directly to those who have triumphed in the madhouse world of modern business ("To those who have taken the opportunity to advance") and offers "an opportunity to retreat" into a quasi-pastoral "sanctuary" in which the conveniences of modern technology emulate a beneficent nature. Like the speaker in Andrew Marvell's seventeenth-century pastoral poem "The Garden," the driver of the Lexus is likely to exclaim: "What wond'rous Life in this I lead!" In Marvell's garden beneficent nature explodes with a cornucopian excess:

> Ripe Apples drop about my head;
> The Luscious Clusters of the Vine
> Upon my Mouth do crush their Wine;
> The Nectaren, and curious Peach
> Into my hands themselves do reach.

In the Lexus, among all the technological marvels in abundance, "the steering column automatically lowers itself" into the driver's hands like Marvell's "Nectaren, and curious Peach."

## SATURN'S PEACEABLE KINGDOM

Throughout the pastoral tradition, the idyllic, healthful, unspoiled natural countryside stands in contrast to the confining, dangerous, artificial city.  An ad campaign for the Saturn line of cars has consistently evoked this version of the pastoral, as the manufacturer (General Motors [GM]) attempted to convey a distinctive image for its first new line of cars in nearly fifty years, even before the car was generally available. According to advertising columnist Beatrice Kanner, writing in *New York* magazine in 1991, just as the car was being launched, GM, attempting to counter the increase of Japanese automobile imports, evoked rural Americana as the dominant image associated with its new vehicle. Unlike the car ads of the mid-eighties, which, as Todd Gitlin has noted, emphasized the power, virility, and mobility of postmodern corporate America ("We Build Excitement"), the Saturn campaign, developed by the same agency (Hal Riney & Partners) that had produced a number of soft-focus, lush ads for such products as Gallo Wine and Bartles and Jaymes wine coolers, as well as Ronald Reagan's famous "It's Morning in America" election campaign spots, began with a series of ads that tied the Saturn to traditional American values such as family and community. The plant Saturn built in rural Tennessee was the primary focus, and the ads emphasized that this was a car that was at once innovative and new and also as "old as the hills." The workers were solid American types with families and pets, recapturing the American past, pre-1960, of small-town homely values and craftsmanship. As Kanner describes one ad, the autoworker featured (portrayed by an actor) "poignantly recalls the glory days of the sixties—shattered by the oil embargo—and talks about his recent decision to 'start a clean slate'" in the lush hills and valleys of the South, shots of which are intercut with images of the worker's lined and rugged face. In another ad, a young boy, transplanted with his family, presumably from the industrial North, worries about adjusting to his new home and making new friends until he discovers the joys of being a newspaper delivery boy—the quintessential small-town childhood idyll. These ads convey a sense of solidity and pride in workmanship (to counter the perception that American vehicles lack these values) and suggest that the cars are individually crafted by dedicated workers and not merely put together by faceless bodies (both human and robot) on an assembly line. The company is not merely another version of corporate America (the connection to GM is suppressed in the ads), but "a different kind of company"—presumably comprising caring, nurturing individuals interested more in the well-being of its workers and the customer and the future of America than in the bottom line—themes the company's ads have continued, culminating in an old-fashioned camp-meeting, family-style "reunion" of customers and employees in the summer of 1994. The campaign was a success; in 1992, the *New York Times* reported a surge in Saturn sales at the expense of Japanese imports.

In later ads for Saturn—which, despite its claims to newness, automotive columnists have noted, bears a strong resemblance to other GM lines—the rural Americana theme continues. Now the emphasis is on the car itself and what it means for its owners. The main themes are safety, reliability, and ruggedness, all values that evoke a mythic American past. While the features the ad copy stresses could be claimed for any vehicle being sold today, the ads try to suggest the distinctiveness of the Saturn by associating it with colorful American indivdualists.

If these unusual people can find the car appealing, it must be special. One character is Velma Willarson of Winchester, Wisconsin, who at seventy-six years of age, drives around with fifty pounds of birdseed in her trunk feeding "hundreds of . . . wild birds out of the goodness of her . . . heart" (Figure 2). Dressed in peasant blouse and skirt with a straw hat pushed back on her head, Velma stands in the ad photo (which ran in *The New Yorker* in November 1991) next to her car, surrounded by bird feeders and sacks of feed and corn. The ambience is rural America, close to nature, and Velma is in communion with the birds. The ad evokes the image of the peaceable kingdom made famous by the primitive nineteenth-century American paintings of Quaker artist Edward Hicks that depict the harmony of man and beast, the reconciliation of the lion and the lamb that obtained in Eden (Figure 3). Similarly, in another 1991 spread, John Holtkamp, a photographer somewhere in the Midwest, is at one not only with the rural milieu he photographs during the week (he is shown "at work" near a corn silo and corn fields), but also with the animals he owns, although they are not the usual barnyard denizens ("the Holtkamps have a llama, eight miniature donkeys, and an emu") (Figure 4).

## NOSTALGIA AND THE PASTORAL

The pastoral is deeply infused with nostalgia, as Laurence Lerner reminds us, and nostalgia informs a wide range of advertising in recent years. As civilization becomes complex and increasingly crisis-ridden, the yearning for a simpler past becomes stronger. In postmodern America, that simpler past is most often identified with the rural life of nineteenth-century preindustrial society or with the pioneering life of the westward movement. The cowboy, the farmer, and the New England peddler have emerged as icons associated with that past, selling cigarettes (Marlboro, embodied in the ubiquitous and long-lived Marlboro Man), cereal (Quaker Oats oatmeal, whose longtime spokesman was character actor Wilfred Brimley, known for a series of grandfatherly rural roles in films and TV series), and cookies (Pepperidge Farm, represented by a wise old peddler traveling about in a horse-and-buggy delivery wagon). Jackson Lears calls this the "rhetorical appropriation of the preindustrial past," a feature of much early advertising. "No matter how fervently they chanted the gospel of newness," Lears writes, "[1920s] advertisers knew they had to establish some common ground, some sense of old-shoe familiarity between the purchaser and the product." They did this through invoking folk icons, which "allowed the adepts of progress to have it both ways: to assert that the best of traditional values survived even as modernization whirled ahead at full tilt. . . . [T]he innovator presented himself as the traditionalist at heart" (385).

The Marlboro Man is probably one of advertising's major contributions to popular culture. Evoking the archetype of the frontier, a series of rugged men have populated the brand's ads consistently since the 1950s, when the product was

VELMA WILLARSON wanted something that could fly down the highway with a fifty-pound load of birdseed.

Ask any rosebreasted grosbeak or nuthatch around Winchester, Wisconsin, and they'll tell you about Velma. She feeds them and hundreds of other wild birds out of the goodness of her 76-year-old heart. They'll tell you how they used to watch her struggling to lift big bags of birdseed out of the back of her old sport coupe.

But no more.

Now Velma's got a brand new Saturn. It not only has a roomy, convenient trunk, but back seats that fold down. Meaning, to everyone's benefit, an increased birdseed-per-trip efficiency.

They'll also tell you that Velma's new Saturn is just about as aerodynamic as anything that rolls on the ground can get.

In fact, the only thing they don't seem to like that much is how quiet the Saturn is. When Velma had her old car, they could hear the sound of lunch coming for miles.

But now, she has to honk.

A DIFFERENT KIND OF COMPANY. A DIFFERENT KIND OF CAR.

*If you'd like to know more about Saturn, and our new sedans and coupe, please call us at 1-800-522-5000.*

©1991 Saturn Corporation. Velma Willarson is pictured with a 1992 Saturn SC.

Saturn's own version of the peaceable kingdom theme features 76-year-old Velma Willarson of Winchester, Wisconsin who drives around with 50 pounds of birdseed in the trunk of her Saturn, feeding "wild birds out of the goodness of her . . . heart." Ad by Hal Riney & Partners. Reprinted by permission of Saturn Corporation.

Advertising draws on fundamental myths like that of the pastoral, an Edenic milieu where humanity and nature, man and beast, are in harmony, as in the painting, *Peaceable Kingdom*, by the 19th-century primitive artist Edward Hicks (1780–1849). The Metropolitan Museum of Art, Gift of Edgar William and Bernice Chrysler Garbisch, 1970.

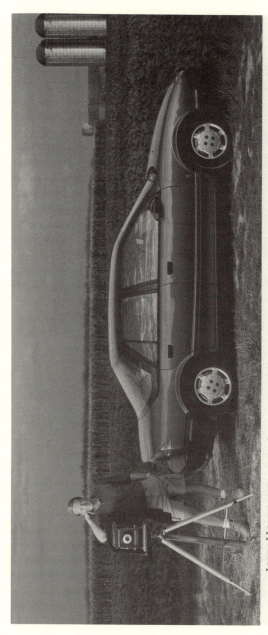

Another Saturn pastoral depicts John Holtkamp, a photographer somewhere in the Midwest, at work in his rural milieu near a corn silo and corn fields. Ad by Hal Riney & Partners. Reprinted by permission of Saturn Corporation.

repositioned from being a "woman's" cigarette of middling success in the market to become the leading brand internationally. So successful is the campaign, with all its redolence of earthiness, ruggedness, and virility, that the ads for the cigarette typically require no body copy to get their message across. The image is all. Brimley's appearance in Quaker Oats ads and the character in the Pepperidge Farm series evoke country common sense and rural rectitude as well as the values of thrift and simplicity associated with the ideals of an earlier American work ethic. In Brimley's ads, whether on TV, where he has been a familiar paternal figure in numerous drama and sitcom series, or in print, the rural nostalgic virtues are embodied in a simulation of an idealized non-urban dialect, marked by elision of initial and terminal consonants. In one ad for "New Cinnamon Toast Oatmeal" that appeared in *Ladies' Home Journal* (Nov. 1991), the forms *'em* and *nourishin'* underscore Brimley's persona of grandfatherly affection as he, looking a lot like Teddy Roosevelt, bewhiskered and with old-fashioned eyeglasses, watches two youngsters eating steaming bowls of the product. Pepperidge Farm's spokesman, the fictional New Englander Titus Moody (actually a creation of the popular Fred Allen radio program in the 1940s, and hence a doubly nostalgic figure) likewise speaks in the clipped and nasal tones of the countryside. These icons impart to the products the virtues of nature, simplicity, and homeyness. All of them, of course, are in reality machine-made by highly rationalized technological companies, often subsidiaries of multinational conglomerates. A *New Yorker* cartoon some years ago playfully summarized this state of affairs, depicting an executive of "Mom's Pies" sitting in his ultramodern office, a huge factory (a subsidiary of some large corporation) visible through the window in the background.

But nostalgia is just as likely to be embodied in the not-so-long-ago world of the 1950s. This is not surprising since the demographically dominant baby-boom generation grew up then. The last age perhaps of small-town virtue, the age of "Ozzie and Harriet," "Father Knows Best," and "I Love Lucy," the fifties embody an aura of innocence and communal good feeling—they are, as Fredric Jameson has called them, "the privileged lost object of desire" for contemporary Americans (19). The complexities of the age, the political turmoil and national crises of Korea and the anti-Communist hysteria, are washed away in a hazy black-and-white TV image of nuclear families living in suburban or urban harmony, where the problems of growing up are solved by good old Dad, who, like Robert Young in the archetypal role of national Father who Knows Best, can coolly carve a Sunday roast in his suit jacket just as easily as he can dispense sage and stern advice to his often fractious children (Miller).

The nostalgia for the fifties informs a number of popular culture products from the 1972 film *American Grafitti*, which, although actually set in the early 1960s, is often credited with launching the trend to pre-sixties nostalgia, to the TV sitcoms that followed in its wake to the continued popularity of reruns of 1950s TV shows on cable TV. Films like *Batman*, *The Addams Family*, and *The Untouchables* recycle old TV plots and characters. Television ads too invoke this fifties idyll, often using black and white clips from shows like "Leave It to Beaver" or imitations of shows like "Dragnet" to sell a variety of products from cars to Yellow Pages advertising.  Ads for the Mazda Miata, a contemporary rendition of the classic open roadster popular in earlier decades, ambiguously evoke a vision of life that looks like the fifties but is in reality now in what has been termed "instant nostalgia."

One of the kings of pastoral nostalgia in ads is fashion designer Ralph Lauren, whose whole mystique is centered on recapturing a lost past that blends inconsistently—or perhaps in postmodern pastiche—cowboy work clothes, upper-class elegance, family values, and exotic adventure.  Lauren's pastoral is not totally equated with the life of rural simplicity, although that is one strand of his fashion vision.  Like many contemporary fashion merchandisers, he has elevated rural utilitarian modes of dress—plaid shirts, blue jeans, work boots, cowboy hats—into a fashion look, done up in rich fabrics that no yeoman at any time in history could have afforded.  Juxtaposed against this look (which is complemented by household furnishings that evoke simple country houses and Shaker furniture design) are the other Lauren worlds of the upper-class idyll, replete with tweeds, tennis sweaters, lavish mansions, and polo matches (Lauren's trademark), and the colonial world of 1930s Africa.  As *New York Times* critic Paul Goldberger states in a retrospective look at Lauren's success as a fashion designer and cultural icon, "In an age in which artifice often seems to become reality, Mr. Lauren has become the ultimate life-style purveyor, the ultimate producer of completely packaged, perfect life" (II, 1). Goldberger attributes much of Lauren's success to the way in which he uses the imagery of the past: "[H]is work does not so much break new ground as reinvent the past, turning it into a siren call—soft, alluring, and absolutely free of blemishes. . . . He is like a great scavenger, scouring the world for images, images he edits and recasts into his own, refined versions" (II, 34).

In the wake of Ronald Reagan's unprecedented landslide reelection in 1984 on the theme of "It's Morning in America," a new wave of nostalgia-laden and patriotic ads swept through American media.  Thus, as Alessandra Stanley noted in the *New Republic* a few years ago, Lauren was the appropriate icon for the political climate of the eighties and early nineties, but he is certainly not alone in evoking the genteel past. The "Morning in America" spots evoked the values of small town life—brass bands, Fourth of July parades, hard work on the land—all in a montage of soft-focus images that had been introduced into television advertising by McDonald's and had been pushed to new heights of evocativeness by the "Reach Out and Touch Someone" campaign of AT&T in the 1970s.

Chronicling the development of the first of AT&T's famous series of ads, Michael Arlen described the attempts of the TV ads' director to achieve a certain look that would permit the viewer, in the brief span of thirty seconds, to "read" the ad on an emotional level. Although Arlen did not directly comment on the images that comprised the ad's montage (a child tap-dancer talking on the phone to her grandfather, a vaudeville performer; a young recruit to the military talking to his father, a barber; a rodeo performer talking to his girlfriend, an equestrienne; a son talking to his hockey-star father), the ad conveys its sense of connectedness through nostalgia-laden imagery. The crew filming the commercial spent much time and effort tracking down locations for the various shots,  rejecting several because they did not "read" well; that is, they did not convey what these places were supposed to look like stereotypically.  Those stereotypical images turn out, perhaps unconsciously, to evoke a by-gone age, an age of vaudeville theaters, rodeos, cluttered barber shops, and military bases.  For the military base scene, the producers spent untold hours tracking down an old phone booth—one that looked like a "real" phone booth—to deepen the nostalgic layers of meaning.

The ads of George Bush, Ronald Reagan's successor, in his 1988 campaign latched onto the same thirst for nostalgia that infused Reagan's campaign and the Lauren aesthetic.  As  Alessandra Stanley described them in her *New Republic* piece, the ads featuring montages of a Bush family picnic at their summer home in Kennebunkport, Maine, resembled "an instant Ralph Lauren advertisement, one of those lush tableaus of well-bred families at play . . . moodily evoking class and quality and grace" (18). This was the same George Bush, of course, who was also attempting to cultivate a populist image to downplay his elite upbringing as the scion of a politically and socially prominent family with a Yale education.  No matter that the Lauren imagery ("Tradition. Family. Manners," as Stanley summarizes its essence) stood in opposition to the pork rinds, the country music, and the rough-and-tumble Texas oilfields that Bush evoked on the campaign trail. In many ways they both go back to powerful strands of national myth.

As the national myth has become contested ground in the ongoing political debate that many have defined as a "culture war" (Hunter), the idyllic images of America's past—our pastoral inheritance—have been invoked more vigorously in subsequent campaigns.  In the 1992 campaign all three candidates for President (Bush, Clinton, and Perot) defined themselves in terms of small-town values and a nostalgic return to the past. Bill Clinton's campaign made much of his growing up in the symbolically redolent Hope, Arkansas, while Ross Perot's childhood in rural Texas was claimed as the basis for his no-nonsense, straight-talking approach to complex problems.  And in 1994, the Republican congressional upsurge called upon images of the small-town, pre-1960s past as a counterforce to the alleged corruption of the American idyll by 1960s hippies and liberals, a past that historian Richard Lingeman has claimed may never really have existed. The same small town so lovingly evoked by commercials for McDonald's and presidential candidates was the place most Americans fled from.  As Lingeman writes, "Is there any other country where the concept of 'hometown' has such emotional resonance—where so many people anchor their beings in some small town they or their parents fled long ago? . . . Grown men and women secretly harbor a nostalgia for their home place, even though they once thought it suffocating and conformist and lacking in opportunity" (107).

## THE LOGIC OF MYTH

But it is the function of myths, like the myth of the pastoral and its descendant myth of the idyllic small town, to anchor culture in a set of values, whether those values have an objective reality or not. As early twentieth-century investigations of myth from Sir James George Frazer's *The Golden Bough* to the psychoanalytic constructs of Sigmund Freud and Carl Gustav Jung have made clear, myth speaks "a forgotten language" of consciousness, in Erich Fromm's phrase. Myth contains clues to the structure of the unconscious; its imagery (recapitulated in folk and high literature and dreams) expresses the universal desires and fears of humanity no matter where situated temporally or geographically. Myth is the language of the unconscious itself, expressing in its wild, often illogical forms and images humanity's attempts to understand the world it found itself in. Modern society, according to Freud and Jung (especially Jung) and their followers, had become disconnected from the evocative language of myth through the rise of scientific thinking, which condemned mythic expression to the realm of prescientific, naive daydreaming. But the truths of myths were not to be denied; they remained vital for modern humanity to understand, for the lack of understanding could be the cause of the psychic disintegration apparent throughout modern cultures and societies. As Jung wrote in *Man and His Symbols*, a popularization of his system of thought:

Modern man does not understand how much his "rationalism" (which has destroyed his capacity to respond to numinous symbols and ideas) has put him at the mercy of the psychic "underworld." He has freed himself from "superstition" (or so he believes), but in the process he has lost his spiritual values to a positively dangerous degree. His moral and spiritual tradition has disintegrated, and he is now paying the price for his break-up in world-wide disorientation and disintegration. (94)

Thus, the modernist quest to recover the essence of myth was both a quest to recover the spiritual from which modern "man" had been cut off and to reclaim the origins of thought and even language, as the philosophers Suzanne Langer and Ernst Cassirer argued.

Postmodern approaches to myth, albeit less psychologically and religiously oriented than the modernist, are no less thoroughgoing in the attempt to recover the origins of consciousness and the originary ground of human thought. The major postmodernist study of myth, Claude Lévi-Strauss's four-volume *Mythologiques* and the work leading up to it ("The Structural Study of Myth" and *The Savage Mind* [*Pensée Sauvage*]), attempts no less than an unraveling of the logic of mythic thinking as a clue to the nature of mind. In Lévi-Strauss's view, myth occupies a privileged position as a mental operation that provides a system of thought (a mythic-logic) that structures the way in which humans deal with their world and their place in it. Myth is not merely the possession of primitive humanity or the naive expression of prescientific societies, but the ground on which all systems of human thought are built—even modern advertising.

As Varda Leymore  argues, through a Lévi-Straussian reading of contemporary British advertisments, advertising and myth share similar patterns of structure and are "preoccupied with essentially the same problems.  Both strive to provide answers to the eternal polarities of the human condition": life and death, we and they, war and peace, happiness and misery (154).  Advertising, Leymore maintains, functions like myth in being an "anxiety-reducing mechanism": "To the constant nagging dilemmas of life, advertising gives a simple answer.  In buying certain products or obtaining a service, one buys not only a 'thing', but also an image. This image consists of the belief and the hope in something better" (156).

But this is only half the story.  Advertising goes beyond being merely an appropriator of traditional myth, or functioning *like* myth; it is a mythical system in itself.  As  the major vehicle for propagating the values of modern society—as the main carrier of ideology in Louis Althusser's sense—advertising is a primary means by which modern society defines itself. It thus fills the role that Lévi-Strauss identified for myth in primitive culture, reconciling contradictions and providing a definition of the "natural" common sense of the culture. In Roland Barthes' terms, advertising is myth as a second-order semiological system that appropriates meaning from the first order of signification and fits it into a seamless web of ideologically constructed meanings.  Thus, advertising as myth creates a new language of experience that is built on traditional categories and meanings and constructs new language that is "natural" common sense.  In the mythic world of advertising, products displace the world of the spirit. Life becomes defined by the products accumulated or used.   Community, love, family, and religion are expressed through icons of industrial production.  Pepsi is youth and youth is Pepsi, forever frolicking in an Eden of sun-filled streams and beaches, engaging in an eternal baptism of innocence. McDonald's restaurants serve as social centers and nurturing institutions, locales of conviviality, providers of food and drink in never-ending abundance.   Automobiles  enable  an  escape  to  the  isolation  of nature—where there is never any other car or person to be seen—or, as in a recent TV advertisement for Buick, in which autumn leaves are seen falling up to the trees, they can make time run backwards.

In this respect, advertising as myth is integral to the modernist quest. As Perry Meisel argues in *The Myth of the Modern*, the attempted recuperation of origins is *the* ultimate quest of belated modern culture, and the perceived failure of that recuperation stands as modernity's chief anxiety.  Advertising claims to triumph over belatedness and anxiety and to recuperate the originary world through its pastoral imagery.  Like the Adamic couple in Calvin Klein's celebrated ads for his appropriately named fragrance "Escape," ads transport us to Eden from which we hope never to come back.  Advertising brooks no failure; progress is its  most important product, and there is no problem that the products of modern technology can not solve.  It is questionable, however, whether advertising can recover the numinousness of the traditional mythic world; advertising is as powerless as any other aspect of our culture to reclaim origins. The mythic world that advertising substitutes for deeper levels of consciousness, its attempt to throw up a new form of numinosity in the products it sells, by design leaves its consumers unfulfilled, ever questing to reclaim Eden. And as Jacques Derrida taught us some years ago, such a quest remains unfulfilled and unfulfillable, for, as Gertrude Stein might have said, there is no there there.

## NOTE

1. Ironically nature had the last laugh. A severe hurricane in the summer of 1992 inflicted major damage on the island.

## WORKS CITED

Althusser, Louis. "Ideology and Ideological State Apparatuses." *Lenin and Philosophy and Other Essays.* Trans. B. Brewster. New York: Monthly Review Press, 1971.

Arlen, Michael. *Thirty Seconds.* New York: Farrar, Strauss and Giroux. 1980.

Barthes, Roland. "Myth Today." *Mythologies.* Trans. Annette Lavers. New York: Hill & Wang, 1975: 109–159.

Buell, Lawrence. "American Pastoral Ideology Reappraised." *American Literary History* 1 (Spring 1989): 1–29.

Derrida, Jacques. " Structure, Sign, and Play in the Discourse of the Human Sciences." *The Structuralist Controversy.* Ed. Richard Macksey and Eugenio Donato. Baltimore: Johns Hopkins University Press, 1970: 247–265.

Dyer, Gillian. *Advertising as Communication.* London: Methuen, 1982.

Empson, William. *Some Versions of Pastoral.* 1934; rpt. New York: New Directions, 1974.

Fromm, Erich. *The Forgotten Language: An Introduction to the Understanding of Dreams, Fairy Tales, and Myths.* New York: Grove Press, 1957.

Frye, Northrop. *Anatomy of Criticism: Four Essays.* Princeton, N.J.: Princeton University Press, 1957.

Gitlin, Todd. "Car Commercials and *Miami Vice*: We Build Excitement." *Watching Television.* Ed. Todd Gitlin. New York: Pantheon, 1987: 136–161.

Goldberger, Paul. "25 Years of Unabashed Elitism." *New York Times* 2 Feb. 1992: II, 1, 34.

Green, Harvey. *Fit for America.* Baltimore: Johns Hopkins University Press, 1988.

Hunter, James Davison. *Culture Wars: The Struggle to Define America.* New York: Basic Books, 1991.

Jameson, Fredric. *Postmodernism or the Cultural Logic of Late Capitalism.* Durham, N.C.: Duke University Press, 1991.

Jung, Carl G., et al. *Man and His Symbols.* Garden City, N.Y.: Doubleday, 1964.

Kanner, Beatrice. "Orbiting Saturn." *New York* 15 Apr. 1991: 14–19.

Lears, Jackson. *Fables of Abundance: A Cultural History of Advertising in America.* New York: Basic Books, 1994.

Lerner, Laurence. *The Uses of Nostalgia: Studies in Pastoral Poetry.* London: Chatto & Windus, 1972.

Lévi-Strauss, Claude. *The Raw and the Cooked: Introduction to a Science of Mythology I.* Trans. John and Doreen Weightman. New York: Harper & Row, 1969.

Leymore, Varda Langholz. *Hidden Myth: Structure and Symbolism in Advertising.* New York: Basic Books, 1975.

Lingeman, Richard. "A Consonance of Towns." *Making America: The Society and Culture of the United States*. Ed. Luther S. Luedtke. Chapel Hill: University of North Carolina Press, 1992: 95–109.

Machor, James L. *Pastoral Cities: Urban Ideals and the Symbolic Landscape of America*. Madison: University of Wisconsin Press, 1987.

Marchand, Roland. *Advertising the American Dream: Making Way for Modernity 1920–1940*. Berkeley: University of California Press, 1985.

Meisel, Perry. *The Myth of the Modern: A Study in British Literature and Criticism After 1850*. New Haven, Conn.: Yale University Press, 1987.

Miller, Mark Crispin. "Prime Time: Deride and Conquer." *Watching Television*. Ed. Todd Gitlin. New York: Pantheon, 1987: 193–228.

Shi, David E. *The Simple Life: Plain Living and High Thinking in American Culture*. New York and Oxford: Oxford University Press, 1985.

Snell, Bruno. *The Discovery of Mind: The Greek Origins of European Thought*. 1953; rpt. New York: Harper & Brothers, 1960.

Stanley, Alessandra. "Presidency by Ralph Lauren." *The New Republic* 18 Dec. 1988: 18–20.

Williamson, Judith. *Decoding Advertisements: Ideology and Meaning in Advertising*. London: Marion Boyars, 1978.

# 4

# "We Bring Good Things to Life"/"We're Always There": The AdWorld of GE

## Harry Keyishian

General Electric (GE), a company that offers a wide range of products and services, has used institutional advertising consistently and well over the years to claim a key role in shaping modern civilization. Assuming the roles traditionally reserved for religion and patriotism, it has placed itself at the center of a vision of society purged of the ills of postmodernism—alienation, fragmentation, and cultural confusion. While hardly new, institutional advertising—advertising aimed not at selling specific products, but at promoting the identity of an entire company—has gained great prominence in recent years. Like product advertising, it uses tested methods of identification and association to perform its function, but it does so for the purpose of creating respect for institutions rather than desire for particular objects. According to Roland Marchand, the practice of institutional advertising began with AT&T's 1908 campaign to convince the general public of the benefits of private monopoly in the face of populist hostility toward powerful economic institutions (5). It accelerated after World War I, as such firms as Squibb, Metropolitan Life, General Motors, and GE sought to gain public prestige commensurate with their size and influence.

The latter two companies turned to the firm of Batten, Barton, Durstine and Osborn (BBDO) to mount "dignified and highminded" campaigns to manage the creation of their images; and given their purposes, they made a wise choice. Straddling the worlds of religion and commerce, BBDO partner Bruce Barton gained fame as author of *The Man Nobody Knows,* his best-selling 1926 book characterizing Jesus as a publicity-minded businessman (8).

Institutional advertising is designed to articulate corporate values—or what the corporation wishes the public to believe are its values. Here I describe the corporate philosophy and worldview presented in GE's long-running series of television commercials—short films, actually, and produced by BBDO New York since 1979—which embody and illustrate the corporate philosophy set forth in its annual reports to stockholders. I am not concerned here with the question of how closely the GE campaign resembles its actual corporate practice—news accounts of suits brought against the corporation for polluting and other violations[1] indicate the existence of a gap—but rather I will describe the ways the ads enunciate the company's corporate strategy and philosophy.

## SOFT VALUES AND HARD FACTS

Ad critic Leslie Savan has aptly characterized GE's prime motive in its institutional ads as selling America "the paternalistic, everything-under-control world that GE seems to rule" (Savan 8). This pitch follows logically from the picture of itself the corporation presents in its annual reports, especially in the introductory "Letter to Share Holders," signed in recent years by Chairman and CEO John F. Welch, Jr., and Vice Chairman Paolo Fresco. The news in these "Letters" is generally very good—"1992 was another strong year for GE in a difficult global economic environment"; "1993 was a very good year for your Company, a year when our soft initiatives turned increasingly into hard results"—though sometimes bad news filters in: "GE had a great year in 1994, with the notable exception of the Kidder, Peabody issue."

But even that admitted failure (GE was forced to sell at a loss the brokerage house it had bought in 1986) is used to reinforce and validate GE's stated corporate values. Dismissing as "academic" the question of whether the original purchase of Kidder was wise (GE 1994 Annual Report 5), the report ascribes Kidder's failure to overall weaknesses in trading markets and to the wrongdoing of an employee whose phantom trading scheme cost the company $210 million in net income. GE's message to stockholders is that far from discrediting the company's corporate philosophy, this uncharacteristic misfortune merely demonstrates the importance of staying competitive:

The tragedy of businesses that are not market leaders, that don't have a broadly based competitive edge—be they brokerage houses or manufacturing plants—is exactly the same; and it goes beyond "one-time charges"—dollars and cents. It's the people—the factory or office workers—who can't just "go down the street"—like traders and managers can—for another job. This human toll reminds us, once again, that nothing we do is more important than staying competitive—keeping that winning edge. Nothing. (5)

The report adroitly connects the "hard" practice of staying competitive to the "soft" values associated with a concern for its work force.

In GE's 1992 Annual Report, Welch and Fresco sound almost apologetic about the company's ongoing struggle to find an appropriate balance between humane values—"soft concepts"—and business efficiency:

We have produced our fair share—maybe more—of rhetoric over the recent past, discussing soft values with you in this report and struggling among ourselves at all levels of GE to distill just what the characteristics of a winning company are, what makes work exciting and fulfilling rather than just tedious drudgery, and what kind of leadership traits will galvanize and inspire an organization. (GE 1992 Annual Report 1)

They describe their efforts to emulate the creativity of small companies—companies that are "uncluttered, simple, informal," that "thrive on passion and ridicule bureaucracy" and "need everyone, involve everyone, and reward or remove people based on their contribution to winning" (2):

We love the way small companies communicate: with simple, straightforward, passionate argument rather than jargon-filled memos, "putting it in channels," "running it up the flagpole" and, worst of all, the polite deference to the small ideas that too often come from big offices in big companies. (2)

"What we are trying relentlessly to do," they go on, "is to get that small company *soul*—and small company *speed*—inside our big-company body" (3). In particular, they stress the notion of "boundarylessness"—"a way of getting people outside of their organizational boxes and offices and working together, faster" (3)—as means to make GE more efficient and responsive than its competitors.

The body of GE corporate-oriented television commercials created by BBDO New York since 1987 reflects these concepts. In these ads, the company does more than project a set of values; it also positions itself in the larger social context by writing a revisionist history of American culture in which the social good is defined as an extension, and ultimately a product, of its corporate existence and values.

## BRINGING GOOD THINGS TO LIFE

GE's supple signature slogans—"We bring good things to life" and "We're always there"—not only provide a point of closure for their corporate TV commercials: They also suggest that the company's temporal and spatial hegemony guarantees cultural continuity, social interdependence, and metaphysical security. "We bring good things to life" glances back at the ad's text (visual and verbal) and asserts a startling lesson: Not only does GE provide the world with beneficial products and services that would not otherwise exist; it also, punningly, *creates* life: it *endows* things with life. And it empowers the audience, which by a process of identification (and/or the act of purchase) can become part of the creative "we" that defines and enhances life. The ads may additionally suggest that "GE brings good things to *light*"—a reminder that the company make lightbulbs, of course, but also a claim that it illuminates spiritually.[2] "We're always there" is equally supple, meaning not only that the company has an 800 number available twenty-four hours a day to answer consumer questions—it boasts, "We never close"—but also that it has a history: It not only *is* always "there," but it always *was*, throughout history (or at least the past three quarters of a century). "There" also suggests *everywhere*:

GE exists worldwide (Japan and Hungary being the cited examples) to assist in all affirmative and productive aspects of existence.

Two editing modes are employed in these commercials. Some, like "Dan Fox," which narrates the accidental discovery of lexan by a GE employee, are essentially vignettes, using continuity editing to provide narrative flow. Other ads use associative editing, whereby images are juxtaposed to build a set of impressions that suggest a slogan point. "Tapestry," composed of about thirty separate shots, uses association to engage the viewer with images that cumulatively compose its particular theme. Other ads combine both methods, including elements of narrative among associative images.

In aggregate, the commercials summon up a utopian world in which individuals, families, and nations find fulfillment in cooperation rather than conflict, where employees and their managers work happily, confidently, and proudly to achieve mutually beneficial goals. Some ads, like the one titled "Soft Tech CC," address the fact that GE is in fact a group of companies, sharing a logo, but otherwise diverse in their functions and management. What binds them, the ad says—what the logo signifies—is a set of management priorities:

GE is a family of many different kinds of people. And while it may not look like it, they all have the same job. Bringing good things to life.

As another ad puts it, "People helping people; at GE, it's part of everything we do." Thus defined, GE is positioned to superimpose itself upon any image a viewer might have of the good, the true, the valuable, the nurturing, the Edenic. But GE also does a *job;* it can actualize the yearnings it has called into existence. It not only creates an image for itself; it creates an "us" as well.

### SHOWING THAT WE CARE

GE's ads from the late 1980's stressed an idea that the company wishes us to associate with its corporate identity: that all affirmative aspects of life point in a direction and are part of a pattern—specifically, a tapestry—in which each of us has a part. In the ad "Tapestry" (1987), a yearning voice sings about "you and me" walking "hand in hand"; and, as the instrumental portion continues, an announcer adds, "[E]very product and service we provide is the best it can be. . . .to help you reach your dreams." In the ellipsis, a telephone operator at the GE Answer Center is seen helping a customer. At the end, several voices are blended to reinforce the themes: "GE. . . .We bring good things to life. . . .We're always there."

The key word in this sequence is the multivalent *we*, through which identities are in extremely complex ways blurred, defined, redefined, shifted, tied and untied, and given equivalences. Before we can appreciate that strategy, however, we need to take into account the images that accompanied this text. There are 26 in all, and very brief, as follows:

1. Two young men push an old Volkswagen Beetle down a road to get it started; they exchanges waves with the driver as he pulls away.
2. Two male campers carry a canoe at dawn.
3. A nurse (female) helps a boy rise from a wheelchair.
4. A baby's tiny hand reaches up, hesitates briefly, and then grasps a helping adult finger.
5. A man helps a girl onto a horse.
6. A youngster helps a baby to get dressed; the baby reacts with delight upon seeing the youngster's face again as the shirt is pulled over its head.
7. An elderly woman helps an elderly man up steep concrete steps.
8. A male coach helps a female swimmer.
9. A woman teaches a blind boy to read braille.
10. A GE delivery or service truck leaves a farmhouse; the young farm couple waves good. bye as it rolls down their driveway.
11. An overhead shot shows a financial brochure bearing the GE logo being handed around to a group of men and women at a circular conference table.
12. A nurse aids a patient.
13. A woman operator cheerfully answers a call: "GE Answer Center. May I help you?"
14. A father (white) hugs his bespectacled son.
15. One technician helps another hop into a huge jet engine.
16. The same action, from inside the engine.
17. A (white) doctor or technician hurriedly carting medical equipment is handed a lab coat by a (black) doctor or technician; he waves thanks.
18. Two male scientists (one black, one white) work on a project in a darkened room.
19. A male (white) with a baseball cap opens an oven, from which light flows; a young girl reaches in for the contents.
20. A male chemistry teacher shows an illustration of a crystal structure to a student; this suddenly turns into a great image of the crystal in the sky.
21. A couple walks at sunset with their child.
22. A female telephone operator (black) says cheerfully, "Glad we could help you."
23. A driver wearing a GE cap gives a friendly wave in his side-view mirror.
24. Two male scientists (one black, one white) are in conversation.
25. A satellite is seen in orbit.
26. The GE truck (from shot 10) proceeds farther down the driveway. As it does so, the picture shifts and shrinks as the GE logo appears.

The "we" of the ad is, of course, everyone in it, both those delivering help and those receiving it: "People together helping each other," we are told, "will keep *us* growing strong." Subject and object become identified because aiding others encourages reciprocal action. The "we" who "go hand in hand" are "you and me"—now the singer and the listener, who are substituted effortlessly for the variety of persons in the ad; and, of course, we all make up an "invisible" tapestry—are connected parts of a beautiful social design—whose existence GE has discovered or, by a species of magic, created. Though GE is specifically identified only in shots 10, 11, 13, 22, 23, and 26, it is juxtaposed to a series of benign human interchanges and examples of beneficial technology—sometimes combined, as in shots 15 and 16. Finally, it is asserted that "if *we* show that we care"—for and about each other, and, by implication, about GE's values and the location the ad posits for GE in our lives—we can and will "build dreams that we all can share."

But dreaming is spiritual and speculative, not active and pragmatic; "we" (which now has become the viewer reconstituted in the images and activities the ad presents) will supply the human yearning that unifies and drives the dynamic structure that is society. But it is GE that will actualize these "dreams" because it alone has the resources to do so. GE identifies itself simultaneously with the "we" of the song and as the facilitator of "our" aspirations. It is our function to dream and GE's to make the dreams shareable.

Judith Williamson's perspective on this is helpful. She observes:

Advertisements are selling us something else besides consumer goods: in providing us with a structure in which we, and those goods, are interchangeable, they are selling us ourselves. (13)

But the selves they sell us are ones they have created, and for their own purposes: selves that valorize the role of the organization or manufacturer who has at considerable expense produced and broadcast the ad:

In constituting you as part of a group, advertisements must nevertheless address you as an individual . . . . This appellation [i.e., "hailing"] itself involves an exchange: between you as an individual, and the imaginary subject addressed by the ad. For this is not "you," inherently; there is no logical reason to suppose that the advertisement had "you" in mind all along. You have to exchange yourself with the person "spoken to," the spectator the ad creates for itself. (50)

That spectator has been given a distinct role to play in GE's ad universe—a role, the ads work to convince us, that we have chosen for ourselves, and wisely; one that is in harmony with nature and compatible with a range of referent systems in which we have already invested deeply: family values, personal loyalty, gratitude, charity, religion (with its miracles), tradition, and independence. In life, these elements may often be incompatible or in conflict; the GE ad world brings them into harmonious, stable order for those willing to occupy the subject position the ads create for them.

## PAST, PRESENT, FUTURE

In the world of GE ads, history began in 1918, when, according to a 1990 sixty-second commercial entitled "Pike's Peak," "a small team of GE engineers set a new high altitude record for an aircraft engine. What made it unusual," the voice-over announcer points out, "was that they did it without an airplane." On screen in a dramatic reenactment of the event that uses grainy black-and-white photography to give the ad a documentary look a dozen or so men struggle to push a horsedrawn wagon containing an airplane engine up a mountain. The sheer physical effort required to overcome adverse conditions is stressed:  There is no proper road up the mountain, but only ruts in mud;  the wagon nearly falls apart; the men struggle to control both the horses and the weight of the engine.  Long shots, medium shots, and close ups convey both individual effort and its larger context.  The announcer points out, "Back then, no airplane could fly high enough to test the new turbo supercharged engine.  So they did the next best thing:  They hauled it 14,000 feet up Pike's Peak."

Having established the quixotic nature of the enterprise, the film begins to individualize some of the men involved.  Their eyeglasses suggest that they are bookish and know their way around a lab;  but they are also rugged, as their leathery faces, husky builds, and outdoors garments--boots and leather coats—indicate.  They wear a variety of headgear, inclusing a period-style aviator's cap, complete with goggles.  (What good would it be to test an aircraft engine without a pilot around?).  These are men's men, representing a generation less insulated from nature and from physical effort than our own;  they are our strong ancestors who made the world we inhabit, whose adventures were different from and riskier than ours.  Such images were familiar icons in the movies of the 1930s; their equivalents, serving as visual reference points for contemporary audiences, are to be found in photographic renderings of the Marlboro Man and in recent films like the *Indiana Jones* series.

Getting the engine to the required height is only one stage in the process, however:  next, the engineers try to get it running.  The heroic music that has accompanied the straining men stutters as the engine several times fails to start; trumpets, ready to move on to a victorious cadence, repeat a "ta-*da*" in sympathy with the engineers, to underscore their discouragement and frustration.  The announcer says, "After several fits and starts, this remarkable new engine roared to life"—which, of course, it does at this cue.  Our heroes of the past, who had been downcast at the engine's failure, react with relief and pride in their success.

And this is *our* past, one we are invited to appropriate if we wish, because "it is the same ingenuity and team spirit that has brought GE from the world's first jet engine [here, a quick cut of an early jet plane] to the world's most advanced."  The verbal elisions are significant:  It is *GE* that has come all this way (from the "first jet engine") to "the world's most advanced."  GE has appropriated all that history; history is *its* history, and it can be ours only to the extent we "sign on" to its corporate vision.  Now the commercial shifts to color, to a modern passenger jet, in which, as a young boy looks out the window, a modern pilot announces that the occupants can see Pike's Peak far *below* them.  "Which proves," the announcer says, "when people work together, there's no telling to what heights they can soar." "People" in general—but to be part of history, read that as "GE People," who are the ones who make history happen.

Another significant date in GE history is 1924.  In a 1987 commercial entitled "Baseball," we learn that "[O]n a summer's evening in 1924 in Lynn, Massachusetts, perhaps the most significant game in the long history of baseball was played."  A group of men in business suits, stripped down to vests and shirtsleeves, walk through the streets of a small town carrying bats and gloves in the late afternoon. They have apparently divided into teams and goodnaturedly challenge each other. Even before they get to the field, we know they are not athletes: They are solid, vigorous figures, but a little over the hill. As a small crowd of family and friends gather, they practice through the afternoon, making up with their enthusiasm for their lack of talent. The announcer points out, "It wasn't the pitching that was so extraordinary, nor the hitting; and the fielding—well, it was less than exemplary" (as a thrown ball bounces off a fielder's foot).

"No," he continues, "what made this game truly historic was the time of day–nightfall." Elliptical editing has taken us through the afternoon and into the evening: the "hero" of the film—a smallish man with glasses who has set up outdoor lights at this town ballfield—throws the switch that illuminates the field. The music goes ragtime as the game proceeds, played energetically but without great skill. "It was on this night that this small group of GE engineers ushered in the era of night baseball—baseball under the lights." As with the Pike`s Peak effort, a team of ten or a dozen men does a job whose consequences we can enjoy today. This time, they are named: "And while the names of Hugo Fee and Tommy Perkins and Hank Innes will never be recorded in the Hall of Fame, it was this *earnest band of GE pioneers that made possible for us all the many brilliant nights to come*" (italics added). A quick cut to a present-day ballfield, photographed both at ground level, to show us the far more advanced lighting system, and from high above, to provide a spectacular view of the crowd and players under the lights.

Character is stressed. Though not cast in the heroic mold of their Pike's Peak colleagues—the ballpark engineers are only "earnest"—they get the job done. And again, the documentary spirit is preserved: we are being taught something about our history and encouraged to adopt and admire a set of values—cooperative activity in the service of enterprise and progress. (At the same time, Savan reminds us, "GE hauls us back to the past—before nuclear weapons, toxic wastes, and other stuff they'd rather you not be reminded of" [88].)

The commercial "Dan Fox" focuses on a single individual, but the main protagonist is a cat. "Late one night in 1953, in a darkened GE laboratory a remarkable breakthrough occurred." A cat makes its way through an open window and runs along a table on which various sorts of equipment have been left. It knocks over a beaker and, frightened by the noise it makes as it breaks, runs out. Remaining is the liquid residue, which has hardened around the plastic stirrer that had been stuck into it, creating a hammer-like shape.

"Dan Fox, the young scientist who found it the next morning, had no idea *what he'd created*" (italics added). We see Dan gripping the handle and looking intently at the clear plastic object. He bangs it against a table, drawing the attention of two fellow-scientists. Of the accidently created object we are told that "it was crystal-clear and remarkably strong, even under the most extreme conditions." (Dan, wearing safety goggles and gloves, has baked and frozen the object; staring at it intently, he remains fascinated by its durability.) "It was Lexan, the first of GE's engineered plastics, plastics that would soon make it possible for architects to express themselves more brilliantly;  it would make a car designer's best ideas even better and help doctors in their life-saving work." Each function is illustrated quickly by shots of a molded skyscraper roof, an auto body, and a medical implement.

What lesson to draw from this?  Dan Fox neither hauled an airplane engine up Pike's Peak nor raced around a baseball field at night testing the quality of electric lights.  He simply followed up a laboratory experiment and discovered uses for a product he apparently had not planned to invent.  But he, too, finds a place in GE history: "Because what Dan Fox had discovered was something we at GE had always *believed*: You never know where the next idea will come from or how far it will take you." The point is made by a shot of a large station on the Moon, with Earthrise behind it.  The point is that GE can make something of nothing--of an open window, a cat, and an accident—because it is an institution and a psychic condition that endows people like "Dan Fox" with the power to achieve wonders beyond their individual capacities or intentions.

A more recent ad suggests GE's omnipresence by a circular narrative (reminiscent of the old children's narrative "This is the house that Jack built") that begins with the lighting of a bulb and ends with its extinction, in between identifying a role for GE in a full range of human activities.  An announcer's voice says, as the appropriate images flash by:

This is the hand that turned on the light that lit up the desk where the idea was born for a quieter jet engine that flew the technician who works at the power plant that uses its energy far more efficiently and lights up the city and powers the hospital with its life-saving images where Sam was found healthy in time for the game held under the lights and broadcast to millions by a satellite system designed with precision and shipped by powerful locomotives that passed by a factory that helped build a car with advanced thermoplastics that sits in the drive at the home of Patricia who went to the fridge and got a drink for her dad who turns out the light and puts his young daughter to bed.

The "hand" that turns on the light at the beginning is that of a man in blue shirt who has sat before a computer in his home office where evidently he worked up a noise-reduction device now employed by GE in its jet engines.  The rest of the ad flashes the scenes described—Sam is a black youth pronounced well by the magnetic resonance imager—and returns for the final vignette in which a girl of three or so years brings her father a drink, as he works late at his computer, and he puts her to bed.  A second announcer rounds off the account:  "Every day GE technology touches the lives of just about everybody."  GE manifests itself through a range of activities and products and the ad creates us as an audience necessarily implicated at some point in that comprehensive circle.

That GE's scope also reaches beyond American borders is indicated in the commercials "Hungarian Rhapsody" (1990) and "We Make Your Daughters Dance" (1992) about contracts GE has held with companies in Hungary and Japan. Alternatively using candlelight and electric lights as motifs suggesting the new liberties of eastern bloc nations, the former dwells on the idea of freedom:

"Freedom is everything," says one earnest Hungarian; "I feel young again," says another. A succession of images of ballerinas, folk dancers, waltzers in a grand ballroom, and a candlelight procession—as Savan points out, "ye olde Hungary, a lush, pre-commie one awash in royalty" (Savan 147)—suggests universal delight and revitalization in a nation formerly darkened by tyranny and now lit by freedom and technology.

The commercial set in Japan refers to GE's role in building a turbine that provided electric service to the Japanese in Tokyo—and, the ad reminds the viewer with a shot of a smiling black worker, provided jobs for Americans. The format of the ad suggests that its American audiences are viewing an ad made for the Japanese: Over images of Japanese life (quick shots of Kabuki and other forms of theater and dance, families bathing, a baseball game, children meeting their grandparents at a railroad station, etc.), a song is sung in Japanese, while its lyrics about bringing good things to families are translated in subtitles. This song, sung in English (with minor variations), was featured in the first BBDO ad in the "We bring things to life" campaign, made in 1979. Now, as GE spreads its influence, the song is being sung to the Japanese, who have by their association with the company become part of the GE tapestry. The announcer comments:

The people of Tokyo, like people everywhere, know their future depends on getting more electricity in a cleaner and more economical way. To get it, they turned to GE, the world leader in gas and turbine technology. When Tokyo Electric Power gave GE our greatest export order ever, it gave Tokyo the most efficient power plant of its kind in the world. That means more jobs for our people at home. And a better future for the people of Japan.

The mutuality of the benefits incurred by the contract is stressed, and as usual, associative shots—shots depicting general activities—are interspersed with shots that specifically identify GE. In one series, Japanese and American engineers (the Japanese in blue lab coats, the Americans in white), meet and bow to each other in a ritual gesture that shows GE "understands" Japan and its customs, which are at once familiar and exotic.

The theme of universality is carried even further in more recent commercials. In the 1991 ad, "Going Places," a singer rapidly runs off a list of countries where GE products and services are used (each country illustrated in quick cuts). In "One World" (1994), the question, "What are we doing here?," is asked over a series of shots of Asian peoples and then answered: "It's perfectly clear: We're bringing you power"; "saving lives, shining lights"; "power systems, day and night." The capping points are these: "We bring good things to all the world; we bring good things to life."

### "WE BRING ... LIFE"

Additionally GE appropriates to itself power over life and death through the medical technology it has developed. A 1989 commercial, "Excuses," concerns a breast cancer detection system it has developed that promises to detect tumors earlier than any other diagnostic tool and thereby raise survival rates significantly. In the course of the ad a variety of women are heard giving excuses for not keeping medical appointments, intercut with shots of the doctor waiting for them in an empty lab. While claiming its part in averting illness, GE chides women for not living up to their responsibilities in the process: "There's one thing we can't do; we can't make you go."

The implicit claims for the magnetic resonance imager (MRI) are even bolder. In the ad "Prepare a Child" (1989), a boy is escorted through a hospital by his mother. While looking for the room that contains the MRI, they encounter a variety of patients and the boy grows increasingly uneasy, asking finally if he can go home. Meanwhile, an announcer's voice tells us the advantage of the MRI over risky and time-consuming exploratory surgeries. When mother and son get to the MRI, the brave, but worried, child asks the doctor if he can take "Sam," his teddy bear, with him. He and Sam pass through the machine, after which the doctor assures his mother that the condition is "nothing serious."

In another recent commercial, a man of fifty speaks of his sense of sadness caused by a gradual, but unexplained, loss of eyesight. He is seen in a variety of medical examination rooms, with baffled doctors telling him they can find no cause for his affliction. Shots of an attractive family—wife, children, and grandchildren—fade out as the situation is described. The narrator's voice alternates with that of an announcer, who tells the story of his search for help, which he gets when he is examined by the MRI. The MRI alone reveals that the cause of the problem is a hard-to-detect-but-easy-to-treat tumor, and the protagonist is able to see his family clearly again.

In both ads, the patient-protagonist is placed lying face up in an impressive piece of technology that resembles a combination gleaming coffin and torpedo bay. He slides in and then out again in a few seconds (through the miracle of elliptical editing—the imager process usually takes over an hour). In these and other commercials about the MRI the outcome is always the same: The machine discloses that there is no problem after all or else the problem is easily cured. But even that is not the whole story of the MRI: Clearly, the ad suggests, the machine does not just diagnose but also actually *cures.* Patients go in ill and come out well, their diseases healed.

## A BETTER PLACE

Williamson comments, "Obviously [advertising] has a function, which is to sell things to us. But it has another function, which I believe in many ways replaces that traditionally fulfilled by art or religion. It creates structures of meaning" (11-12). In the case of the GE ads described here, that meaning concerns no less than the very existence of meaning, a possibility often denied in the postmodern era. GE provides (i.e., is) the organizing mechanism that by its very existence makes meaning possible. In the words of the 1994 ad "One World," GE is "helping the world go round; we're helping make it a better place, right from our own home town."  What more comforting meaning could GE express than a conviction that the local and the familiar has the power to transform the world and give it purpose?

## NOTES

This essay benefited from suggestions made by the editors of *Journal of Advertising,* for whose help I am grateful.

1. See, for example, Leslie Savan's account of the INFACT documentary *Deadly Deception (*165–168).  The culmination of their long campaign to boycott GE, the documentary describes the devastating effects of radiation leaks from GE nuclear plants in Washington State and New York.

2. Many appliances—ovens and refrigerators especially—glow with a warm, intense spiritual light in GE and other ads.  The symbolism has a history.  Roland Marchand notes BBDO's depiction in the 1930s of GE's electric refrigerator as a "secular icon" (270), full as any cornucopia, which women in print ads showed off  to their enthralled guests: "Sometimes the expressions on the faces of the [fastidiously dressed] women  suggests that they had glimpsed through the opened refrigerator door a secular revelation as spellbinding as any religious vision" (272).

## WORKS CITED

*General Electric Company 1992 Annual Report.*  Fairfield, CT, 1993.
*General Electric Company 1994 Annual Report.*  Fairfield, CT, 1995.
Marchand, Roland. *Advertising the American Dream:  Making Way for Modernity, 1920-1940.*  Berkeley, CA:  University of California Press, 1985.
Savan, Leslie. *The Sponsored Life:  Ads, TV, and American Culture.*  Philadelphia: Temple Univerity Press, 1994.
Williamson, Judith. *Decoding Advertisements:  Ideological Meaning in Advertising.*  London and New York:  Marion Boyars, 1978.

# 5

# Love and Liqueur: Modernism and Postmodernism in Advertising and Fiction

## *Walter Cummins*

Although modernist and postmodernist aesthetics and techniques are usually associated with art and literature, they play a role in contemporary advertising. While the majority of today's advertisements are still premodernist in their assumptions about cause and effect, modernist and now postmodernist ads may be found in growing numbers, usually in media directed toward the young, trendy, and self-proclaimed avant-garde, but occasionally even in the mainstream.

Many of the most revealing are for liquors, perfumes, jewelry, and other expensive luxury items. That is not surprising. Liquors and perfumes promise a glow of intoxication, an overwhelming of inhibitions, while objects of rich luxury lure with another source of transformation, the diamond as a magical charm. French, the fabled (at least to Americans) language of love, also figures prominently in such ads.

The liqueur ads to be discussed below (one for Martell and the other for B and B) appeared in, among other outlets, *The New Yorker*, suggesting that the audience for modernist and postmodernist advertisements must have a certain amount of sophistication and discretionary income.

To illustrate how modernist advertisements and short stories differ from postmodernist, we will consider examples based on the premise of a male-female relationship, perhaps the most familiar source of private and mass cultural fantasies in our age. All of us want fulfilled love for ourselves and for those we identify with, real and fictional.

In the typical premodern version of the story, the frustrations to love are somehow external or at least apart from the authentic mutual core of that love: hostile fathers or misdirected messages or misinterpreted observations as in *Tom Jones*, aggressive self-deceptions as those of Beatrice and Benedict in *Much Ado About Nothing*, false impressions and seeming social barriers as in *Pride and Prejudice*. But for all the frustrations and impediments that drive the plots, love anchors their realities. It is true, genuine, lasting, the source of great meaning. It need only be realized.

Such stories, like most of the premodern, exemplify the principles of literary Realism, which "holds our own actual universe to be one that is finite, orderly, sensible and complete" (Nash 32).[1] Centered on character, Realism assumes that what happens to individuals in stories reveals truths of human nature through dramatization of "meaningful and orderly" experiences (Nash 14). For Realism, "the orderliness of an *unambiguous causal* conception of the universe is essential" (Nash 9). The world described is singular. Through the resolution of the plot, motive and meaning are disclosed, revealed with certainty and lucidity. In short, if before taking an action or making a decision we knew what we learn afterwards, we could control the consequences of our deeds and therefore shape our destinies. Realist stories are in effect cautionary tales.

The advertising examples of this premodern Realist paradigm are countless. Their answers to human dilemmas are clear. All one need do is brush with the right toothpaste, drive the right car, wash with the right shampoo, drink the right beer. The barriers to love have merely been superficial, and the beloved comes to his or her senses once the product has been purchased and applied.

But modernism complicates these relationships by internalizing the impediments to a degree beyond simple ignorance and self-deception. Self-exploration and the resulting self-awareness fail to provide answers that are more than fleeting. Life is in a state of constant process. Other people change, the self changes, love changes. Yet we long for the permanence of premodern love, for love everlasting. Deep down, we know it is out there, often just beyond our reach.

The postmodern story eschews even the hope of stability, undermining all hope for illusions of significance and with them the process of story making that causes such illusions to be so seductive. If subjective choices of details create the drama and meaning of our lives, postmodernism exposes the artificiality of such selection, refusing to let us forget all that has been left out and how including those details would make even the fabrication of coherence impossible. Postmodernism rubs the reader's nose in the arbitrariness of all dramatic shaping.

Brian McHale in *Postmodernist Fiction* contrasts modernism and post-modernism: "[The modernist] world is stable and reconstructible, forming an ontologically unproblematic backdrop against which the movements of the characters' minds may be displayed" (234). For McHale, modernist fiction is essentially epistemological, in contrast to postmodernist fiction, which is ontological (9).[2] Postmodernism asks its ontological questions based on our uncertainty about the world we live in: what worlds exist, how they are structured, what happens if their boundaries are violated, how people relate to the world, what they can do about it (10). It distrusts our capabilities to interpret the context of our lives: what can be known, who knows it, the limits of the knowable, the possibility of reliable transmission of knowledge.

## A MODERNIST STORY

Ann Beattie's short-short story "Snow" provides a concise illustration of the modernist dilemma as defined by McHale.  Only 800 words long, it presents a failed love affair through the memories of a winter together spoken by a woman to a man who is no longer present in her life.  After revealing her version of the experience, she admits that his memories are different and imagines what they must be.  Then she tells of a recent visit to the house they once lived in, reporting that a neighbor had died, his pool shrouded with black plastic, and that only a few white flowers grow in the yard, nothing like the field of snow of their time together.  Finally the narrator, self-conscious that memories are just stories, attempts to break the experience down into mere words; but emotion dominates, and the words of her memory are rich with personal meaning.

The story's core events are ontologically certain.  "Snow" is quite definite that only one external experience exists: The couple shared a house as lovers for a brief winter and then parted.  Their memories of their time together differ because their emotions toward one another, and therefore toward that period of their lives, differ.  However, certain facts of the story are undeniable: They spent a winter together in a specific house, friends visited, a chipmunk got loose in the library, they experienced snowfalls together.  It is the subjective value of these experiences that conflict, the symbolic details that give them different meanings for each participant.  For her, it was a time of joy that she longs to renew; for him, it was just an episode that did not work out.  The narrator is still in love, and he is not.  It is one story from two perspectives.

Her memories are charged with wonder, poetic in their vision: "Remember the night, out on the lawn, kneedeep in snow, chins pointed at the sky as the wind whirled down all the whiteness?  It seemed that the world had been turned upside down, and we were looking into an enormous field of Queen Anne's lace" (287).  The impulse of the story is an implied appeal to the now gone beloved, a monologue that is a plea to recall and relive the bliss of sharing a life in love.

But she is highly aware of modernist subjectivity, that they had very different experiences of the same events: "You remember it differently.  You remember that the cold settled in stages, that a small curve of light was shaved from the moon night after night" (287).  Beattie's narrator also has learned this lesson in story telling, that "[a]ny life will seem dramatic if you omit mention of most of it" (287).

She admits that her memory of the love relationship is a private creation: "This is a story, told the way you say stories should be told: Somebody grew up, fell in love, and spent a winter with her lover in the country" (288).  But this "barest outline" requires fleshing out, details and symbols to give it meaning, at least *her* meaning: "Love, in its shortest form, becomes a word.  What I remember about all that time is one winter.  The snow.  Even now, saying 'snow,' my lips move so that they kiss the air" (288).

Unlike premodern Realism, which claims to depict a single objective world, modernist art is a series of choices, a self-conscious shaping selected from an abundance of alternatives.  We organize meaning because we all want our lives to be a coherent unity, a totalized purposeful narrative, not just a random collection of events.

Linda Hutcheon emphasizes this modernist longing in *A Poetics of Postmodernism*: "Modernists like Eliot and Joyce have usually been seen as profoundly humanistic . . . in their paradoxical desire for stable aesthetic and moral values, even in the face of their realization of the inevitable absence of such universals" (6).  Beattie's narrator, kissing the snow, craves the universal of love; even though literally referring to a snowplow that cleared the "artery" of their road, she acknowledges that metaphorically "neither of us could have said where the heart was" (288).  What concept could be more humanistic than the heart as the source of emotional authenticity?  Despite the modernist sophistication of its technique, "Snow" is a torch song: "My man don't love me and I'm feelin' so blue."

## A MODERNIST AD

Martell cognac's "The Art of Eye Contact" offers a representative example of passion in a modernist ad.  Although its purpose is commercial, meant to sell cognac on the premise that Martell might improve your love life, the ad provides a fruitful text for literary analysis.  The bistro setting feels Parisian; the couple look Latin in hair and features.  The tag line is French: "Cognac. L'art de Martell."  But the mirrored images offer three versions of the same couple, each revealing a different angle of their appearance and—possibly—of their beings.

The woman in the centered unmirrored view, large-eyed and heavy-lidded, seems at the edge of ecstasy, her full lips pursed for a kiss.  Yet mirrored at the left, the eyes appear closed, as if she is asleep.  Or beyond.  With only the front of her face visible—the rest of her head cut off by the man's hair, collar, and vest—her profile is reminiscent of a death mask.  The man unmirrored reveals only the back of his head and a seemingly tender hand barely touching the woman's throat.  But seen to the right in a hazy mirror, his mouth obliterated by a molding, his eyes could be considered fixed and staring, his hand about to reach out and close around her neck.  The gaze, the pose, and the graininess are reminiscent of a silent movie, specifically Rudolph Valentino as the Sheik.  Another more Gallic echo is the stance of Apache dancers, the male threatening violence, the female being a submissive victim.  From that perspective, the pose's angle also suggests the gesture of the vampire, a love that devours.

The ad's copy speaks of a woman's eyes as a reflection of her heart and a man's as a mirror of his soul.  It concludes with a pun that if either needs glasses, they should fill them with Martell cognac.  The clichés about eyes and the strained pun about glasses undercut the photo in two ways.  This woman's eyes are just barely revealed, the bottom edge of a pupil at most; his are seen secondhand, literally mirrored, so that the photo is at least two steps away from his soul.  Note also the eyeglasses on the table, one pair certainly and perhaps a second in the deliberately unfocused photograph,, so that one, maybe both, of the couple lacks 20–20 vision. Though more mobile for passion and possibly more attractive without glasses, that person—deprived of good vision—is not seeing the other clearly.  Myopia and a snifter of cognac accentuate the glow of love.  But is such love only an evening's illusion?

The copy's pun on glasses underlines the possibility of delusion while it undercuts the staged gravity of the couple's pose and the Renaissance symbolism of eyes.  While suggesting that in this day and age optical devices allow us to see clearly, the joke urges the couple to opt for cognac instead and deepen their emotional intoxication.

The Martell ad can be read as parody with its combination of familiar elements—old movies, passion in a Parisian cafe, clichés about eyes.  Fredric Jameson notes the relationship of parody to modernism because "the great modern writers have all been defined by the invention or production of rather unique styles" that are "not likely to be confused with something else" (15).  Parody assumes "that there is a linguistic norm in contrast to which the styles of the great modernists can be mocked" (16).  In this sense, the ad's norms comfort us with the familiarity of shared cultural icons even though the notion of grand passion evokes a sense of irony at the end of the 20th century.  People who drink expensive cognac are too sophisticated to fall for the premodernist ploy that mere use of a product will solve your problems.  However, the advertisers assume they retain a sufficient residue of sentimentality to harbor a fantasy of romantic love and believe beneath their ironic surfaces that alcohol is a path to achieving it.

Although the ad is a singular glimpse into the lives of this fictional couple and not a story with a context in time, it does share similarities with Beattie's "Snow" as an example of modernism.  To use McHale's basic terminology, the setting and the situation are ontologically certain.  It is the subjective interpretation of the scene that is at question.  What does he want of her, she of him?  Is this a one-night stand or a grand passion?  Will he break her heart, or she his?  What do their uncorrected visions see of each other?  How much of their moods can be attributed to the liquor?  Will the woman, like Beattie's narrator, return to the cafe and, instead of kissing air, kiss the rim of a glass?  To use Hutcheon's perspective, the essence of the ad is humanistic in its desire for the stability of true love no matter how much irony tempers the possibility of its fulfillment.

## TWO POSTMODERN STORIES

Like Beattie, Margaret Atwood in "Happy Endings" is very conscious of story telling, but her speaker, who never uses "I," is the writer rather than a character. These contrasting narrators illustrate the fundamental shift that occurs from modernism to postmodernism.  Beattie's "I" is a woman attempting to recapture an interlude of her own life, knowing that her own memory is selective, that she has chosen her metaphors and created her private version of events.   But her involvement is deeply emotional, and her longing is to make her version a reality. Atwood's speaker is detached, a maker of someone else's stories speaking directly to her audience about the mechanics of her trade like a magician revealing step by step the sleight of hand behind the illusion.

Modernism wants readers to immerse themselves in the textures of the fiction at hand and believe that it is truly happening, that the words on the page are revealing living people engaged in the complexities of authentic lives. Henry James tells his stories through the mind of a central intelligence; James Joyce suggests the artist should be "refined out of existence, indifferent, paring his fingernails" (482); even D.H. Lawrence on occasions when he harangues his reader embeds that message in the urgency of his fiction. But in "Happy Endings," Atwood, though usually a modernist, gives centrality to the author, her characters mere names in a series of possible permutations:

John and Mary meet.
What happens next?
If you want a happy ending, try A. (55)

Atwood offers us the choices of versions A through F, six stripped-down summaries of the lives of John and Mary as a couple or as complicated by the appearances of Madge, James, and Fred. Each alternative is very different from the others.

In happy ending A, everything works out perfectly—love, sex lives, children, finances, friendships, vacations, retirement. A happy marriage till their eventual deaths. Version B is reminiscent of "Snow" in that the love is one-sided, Mary for John. John just uses Mary sexually and treats her with indifference while he sees another woman, Madge. Mary, in despair, attempts suicide to make John repent and marry her; but she dies, and "John marries Madge and everything continues as in A" (57). In version C, a middle aged John married to Madge falls in love with a much younger Mary, who tolerates their affair only because her true love, James, is a free spirit away on motorcycle jaunts. When John discovers Mary and James in bed, he murders them and commits suicide in his despair. Madge eventually marries "an understanding man called Fred and everything continues as in A, but under different names" (58). Version D shifts to Madge and Fred, their lucky escape from a great tidal wave that drowns thousands, and their eventual continuation of the happy life of A. In version E, Fred has a bad heart and an understanding marriage to Madge, who "devotes herself to charity work" (58) after his death, although the author offers a variation of this option. Version F makes John a revolutionary and Mary a counterespionage agent, who end up with the lives of A after "a lustful brawling saga of passionate involvement, a chronicle of our times, sort of" (59).

The author then reminds us that the endings of all the versions are the same: John and Mary die. That is the only authentic ending; any other is fake. McHale calls postmodernist fiction "above all illusion-breaking art; it systematically disturbs the air of reality by foregrounding the ontological structure of texts and of fictional worlds" (221). Jean-François Lyotard, a primary definer of the concept of postmodernism, speaks of a postmodern artist "impart[ing] a stronger sense of the unpresentable": "Finally, it must be clear that it is our business not to supply reality but to invent allusions to the conceivable which cannot be presented" (81).

"Happy Endings" concludes with an indication that the whole exercise has been a lesson in story telling, one about plots, "which anyway are just one thing after another, a what and a what and a what" (59). But the story's final sentence reminds us that there are other lessons: "Now try How and Why" (59).

Atwood is clearly having fun with this story, very likely at the expense of postmodernism because she is an author committed to delving into the depths of How and Why, while postmodernism typically eschews such considerations as an unauthentic attempt to impose meaning on a random series of Whats.

Stephen-Paul Martin, a consistently postmodern fiction writer, depicts a confrontation of a man and woman in a story of just several hundred words called "Gallery." The relationship lasts no longer than four brief exchanges of dialogue. The man enters a Houston Street gallery to get out of the cold, sees the woman as they face the same painting, says he does not like it, and is told by her that she painted it. They say a few things about artistic judgment and flirt. He finally asks if she really painted the picture, and she says no. The story closes: "He thought about how cold it was, thought of his mouth between her thighs, felt the weight of words against his teeth, and went outside" (451).

The story depicts a world without certainty, without warmth, a place of isolation and desolation. Key is the notion of the weight of words, for most of "Gallery" is taken up by three long metaphoric series that attempt to convey the meanings of the gestures and innuendos behind their exchanges through sets of analogies to realms and situations far from the setting of the art gallery:

Her tone was like a waitress in a luncheonette in Phoenix, or like a bird that can't survive outside the cage it lives in, or like a zeppelin passing over Big Sur in an earthquake, an intercepted pass in a former hippie's acid flashback, a man rewriting Harry Truman's memoirs, a student coming to class in a baseball uniform, a cosmic revelation based on a misread verse in the Bible. (451)

Of course, these catalogues of similes are meaningless, offering no illumination of her tone or his face or her words. They are only collections of words that have nothing to do with the characters, perhaps interesting in themselves, in the rhythm of their delivery, but giving not a clue as to any How or Why that might explain the meanings of this male-female encounter.

McHale emphasizes the dilemma of language in postmodernism, words as a counterforce to an elusive physical reality rather than a means of elucidation: "[In postmodernist fiction] there is no stable world *behind* this consciousness, but only a flux of discourse in which fragments of different, incompatible realities flicker into existence and out of existence again, overwhelmed by the competing reality of language" (234).

Atwood's "Happy Endings" is ultimately comic because it implies the possibilities of Hows and Whys that give more significance to our lives than an ending in death. Martin's "Gallery," though comic in its details, leaves a much more disturbing impression: the impossibility of creating human connection or communication and of penetrating the Hows and Whys.

Jameson's contrast of modernist parody with postmodernist pastiche provides an insight into Martin's technique of combining references to a myriad of sources. Because, according to Jameson, postmodernism no longer believes "in the existence of normal language, of ordinary speech, of the linguistic norm," it has "nothing but stylistic diversity and heterogeneity. . . . That is the moment at which pastiche appears and parody has become impossible. . . . Pastiche is blank parody, parody that has lost its sense of humor" (16).

Both Atwood and Martin present multiple worlds, Atwood through her contrasting plot outlines, Martin more radically through the range of his metaphors.

## Stephen-Paul Martin

## GALLERY

More to get out of the cold than anything else, he stepped inside a gallery near Houston Street. She caught his eye. Soon they were next to each other facing a painting.

"I don't like this one very much," he said.

"I'm the one who painted it," she said.

Her words were like an abandoned eight-lane highway, like a bear in a small suburban zoo in Oregon, like a frisbee floating six feet over someone's outstretched hand, a small canoe concealing guns on the Nicaraguan border, a robot doing someone's job, a box of unsent letters, a fifteen-page report that gets a "D" in high school physics, someone's basement filled with bubbling tubes and twinkling alembics, a wolf badge kept in a massive eighteenth-century carved oak dresser, a labyrinth drawn form memory on a greasy luncheonette napkin, a resume made from a falsified past, a poplar filmed in Paris, nineteen words crossed out in a debutante's diary near Annapolis, a baby whale whose mother's just been killed, a missing pronoun, a case of laryngitis kept in check with homemade soup, a group of one-celled animals in a petri dish in Munich, a bayonet flashing near the Golan Heights in a beautiful sunset, a silhouette of a silo caught in a photograph in Kansas, or like the sound of change in someone's pocket.

"Oh!" he said. "Well, you know, I don't really know that much about art. Maybe there's some sort of hidden meaning in this picture and I just can't see it."

She laughed and stood a bit closer: "People who don't know much about art are the only ones worth talking to."

His face was like a disappearing staircase, like a beartrap in the Yukon, like a tax deduction no one thinks about claiming, like a wino in the White House, a brand-new constellation, a marvelous group of words that lose their meaning in translation, like three drunks reminiscing about Iwo Jima, a tapeworm in a hologram, reporters watching a pit-bull fight in a millionaire's back yard, an avalanche in the Andes, a knife in a starlet's purse, huge amounts of money not being spent on a cure for AIDS, a former avant-garde artist making millions doing commercials, a baby carriage left out in the rain, a counterfeit penny, a parakeet with a hearing aid, a boxing match in Biloxi, a synonym for distance, the President's balloons beside his bed in a small black table, a beagle by itself in a massive ballroom, a rock star jerking off with the Book of Job in bed beside him, someone's tongue cut out and flown to Wheeling, West Virginia, a woman feeling great who's unaware she's about to get fired, yet another survey showing TV kills intelligence, or the latest set of Pentagon lies that everyone believes in.

"Wow," he said. "Are you serious?"

She took his arm and smiled again: "I always am.  It's funny: I don't like fooling around unless it matters."

Her tone was like a waitress in a luncheonette in Phoenix, or like a bird that can't survive outside the cage it lives in, or like a zeppelin passing over Big Sur in an earthquake, an intercepted pass in a former hippie's acid flashback, a man rewriting Harry Truman's memoirs, a student coming to class in a baseball uniform, a cosmic revelation based on a misread verse in the Bible, a thirteenth-century map of Abyssinia, a broken walkie-talkie in a graveyard near Manilla, a boy who fails a test as a way to show anger toward his parents, a talent scout with an eating problem getting lost in the everglades, an early bird becoming a worm, a camera left in a phone booth, a thumbtack left on a teacher's chair, a urine test in Capetown, a clever bitchy phrase that sells designer jeans by the millions, a fact that's widely known but not quite true, a jar of moonlight, a marvelous meal destroyed by a fight about Coleridge and Wordsworth, an opera fan who finds her favorite singer chained in a sex-club, a boy misspelling bear in a spelling bee, a clock of passion, a biplane losing altitude in the Rockies.

"You really did this picture," he said.

"No," she said.

He thought about how cold it was, thought of his mouth between her thighs, felt the weight of words against his teeth, and went outside.

*Reprinted with permission of the author*

McHale gives metaphor a central role in postmodernism's illusion-breaking:

Postmodernist writing seeks to foreground the ontological *duality* of metaphor, its participation in two frames of reference with different ontological statuses. This it accomplishes by aggravating metaphor's inherent ontological tensions, thereby slowing still further the already slow flicker between presence and absence. All metaphor *hesitates* between a literal function (in a secondary frame of reference) and a metaphorical function (in a "real" frame of reference); postmodernist texts often *prolong* this hesitation as a means of foregrounding ontological structure. (134)

If postmodernism will not allow the world to be pinned down, it can not abide the equivalent conception of individual identity. The reality of the individual is as questionable as that of his or her context. Atwood's characters are only names put through a sequence of experiences. Martin's lack names, knowledge of one another, and even the possibility of a comparison that helps to locate them. All we know about the man is that he is cold and has a sexual impulse, about the woman that she dissembles and may or may not have painted a picture. These presentations do not allow the reader to empathize with their individual emotional experiences, as with the sense of loss felt by Beattie's narrator. The aesthetic reaction is to the stylistic rendering of so many uncertainties, their inventiveness in denying us meaning.

Jameson emphasizes the crucial role of the conception of a unique self for modernist aesthetics in generating a "unique vision of the world" and a "unique, unmistakable style" (17). But for postmodernism, the construct of the self "is merely a philosophical and cultural mystification which sought to persuade people that they 'had' individual subjects and possessed this unique personal identity" (17). Beyond denying the integrity of the self, postmodernism refuses, in Hutcheon's words, "to posit any structure of what Lyotard . . . calls, master narrative—such as art or myth—which, for such modernists, would have been consolatory. It argues that such systems are indeed attractive, perhaps even necessary; but this does not make them any the less illusory" (6).

Postmodernism would seem to be antithetical to advertising and its basic values of stimulating sales and profits. From such a perspective, advertising itself could be a target of postmodernist demolition. Yet there is a view that considers all advertising (as distinct from specifically postmodernist ads) as playing a essential role in the transformation to postmodern culture.

Although referring to the market for works of art, Lyotard emphasizes that postmodernism reenforces consumerism: "[T]his realism of the 'anything goes' is in fact that of money; . . . Such realism accommodates all tendencies, just as capital accommodates all 'needs,' providing that the tendencies and the needs have purchasing power" (76).

E. Ann Kaplan distinguishes a utopian and a commercial postmodernism, the latter analyzed by Jean Baudrillard among others as the result of new technologies that have led to a multinational stage of capitalism in which there is no distinction between high and popular culture, inside and outside, public and private. With the TV screen as the primary reality, this "new, unidimensional universe" permits no escape and offers no opportunity for a critical perspective (4–5). In this world, advertising is a root source of what Jameson identifies as postmodernism's "transformation of reality into images, the fragmentation of time into a series of perpetual presents" (28). Lyotard uses a cultural olio of consumer products to illustrate the postmodern "eclecticism" that "is the degree zero of contemporary general culture: one listens to reggae, watches a western, eats McDonald's food for lunch and local cuisine for dinner, wears Paris perfume in Tokyo and 'retro' clothes in Hong Kong; knowledge is a matter for TV games" (76).

While many of the commentators and theoreticians of postmodernism tend to consider the phenomenon as either a liberating breakthrough or a threat to civilization as we know it, some are not as enthusiastic or as fearful as they place the movement within the continuity of the history of ideas.

Hutcheon sees postmodernism as arising from the issues of modernist humanist assumptions in what she considers the most basic statement of postmodernism's paradox:

Postmodernism questions centralized, totalized, hierarchized, closed systems: questions, but does not destroy. . . . It acknowledges the human urge to make order, while pointing out that the orders we create are just that: human constructs, not natural or given entities. . . . It is a question of commonly accepted values of our culture (closure, teleology, and subjectivity), a questioning that is totally dependent upon that which it interrogates. (41–42)

Sharing certain "modernist strategies: its self-reflexive experimentation, its ironic ambiguities, and its contestation of classic realist representation" (43), "postmodernist contradictory art still installs that [modernist] order, but it then uses it to demystify our everyday processes of structuring chaos, of imparting or assigning meaning" (7).

Even if our processes for contriving structure are exposed, as in Atwood's revelation of the authorial process in "Happy Endings" or in the failed metaphors of Martin's "Gallery," we can not live without the illusion of meaning. Advertising therefore fills the vacuum created by demystification, but can not use the old naive technique of the promised Realist cause-effect connection of product and fulfillment. The postmodernist audience is too jaded for such simplifications even while unwilling to abandon its quests for value, or at least gratifications.

## A POSTMODERN AD

The B and B advertisement "B.Y.O.B&B au mariage" exemplifies a post-modern ad. Its overall effect is spontaneous, arbitrary, *de trop*, contradictory. It is an example of Jameson's notion of pastiche as blank parody because its assemblage of images refers to no precedent and makes no commentary on any original. Its essential irony illustrates McHale's point of an overlapping of worlds and offers no answer to the significance of such a juxtaposition, only a range of possibilities, with no more evidence for one than for any other.

A bride—or at least a young woman in a bridal gown—dominates the picture. One hand holds a bridal bouquet; the other extends a bottle of B and B, the only object in color in the black-and-white photograph. Unbridelike, she wears sunglasses and is stockingless and barefoot. Smiling, her skirt billowing, her veil floating, she runs along the water's edge of a sandy beach. The only other people are two blurred figures behind the bride and made much smaller by this perspective. Their sex is indeterminate; they are overweight and shapeless in garish shirts and dark pants; they give the appearance of middleaged blobs. They appear to be staring at the bride in her youthful joy. Missing from the picture is the groom.

Of course, the bride could be rushing toward him with the offering of B and B, proposing a private celebration. But why aren't they at the reception? Is the reception over and she arrived on their honeymoon without changing clothes? Or has she fled the altar, absconding with a bottle of liqueur and toasting her liberation? Instead of the traditional catered marriage with its abundance of liquor and hors d'oeuvres, this bride brings her own as if to an informal gathering of friends. Perhaps this woman is arriving at a beach party in costume and the marriage referred to is that of the liqueur itself.

No matter what is happening in this scene, a wedding or a beach party, the woman is standing tradition and convention on their heads. She is behaving unsuitably for a wedding and is dressed unsuitably for a party. But from the spirit of the photo, it does not matter. This conjunction of worlds has become a realm with no rules, where anything goes because there are no norms. Married, single, apart or together, drink B and B and feel the happiness of a bride, real or pretend.

But the subtext of the ad suggests that the joy is only transitory.  The middle aged witnesses stand as momenta mori.  The attractive young woman will someday lose her shape and her sexuality.  Nothing is permanent.  Seize the day?

Lyotard stresses the conundrum of knowing for sure: "A postmodern artist or writer is in the position of a philosopher: the text he writes, the work he produces are not in principle governed by preestablished rules, and they cannot be judged according to a determining judgement, by applying familiar categories to the text or to the work" (81).

Ultimately all postmodern art, like this ad, may be playful no matter how serious its philosophical message of the impossibility of achieving any meaning that is not contrived.  Intellectual seriousness is not the same as emotional seriousness.  Readers can share an involvement with Beattie's unhappy narrator as she kisses the absent snow or with the emotional intensity of the couple in the Martell ad.  But in a world where metaphor fails, following the example of the woman on the beach, it is difficult not to make everything a game.

Unlike premodern advertising, which offers implicit rules and categories for achieving our life's goals, postmodern advertising questions our ability to make any sense of our lives.  Still it is selling a product, and the questioning is a cause for smiles rather than despair.  If B and B will not give meaning to our lives, at least it will make the game of living more pleasurable.

## NOTES

1. Although Nash defines Realism to attack it as an ontological falsification, his explanation of the approach offers a perceptive delineation of its methods and premises.

2. Linda Hutcheon, rejecting the applicability of either-or alternatives to postmodernism, points out that McHale is one of a group of theorists who contrast modernist epistemology with postmodernist ontology, while another group of theorists reverses the associations (50). While the ultimate philosophic validity of McHale's distinction may be debatable, it provides a useful heuristic for considering specific examples.

## WORKS CITED

Atwood, Margaret.  "Happy Endings" in *Sudden Fiction International*. Robert Shapard & James Thomas, eds.  New York: W.W. Norton, 1989: 55–59.

Beattie, Ann.  "Snow" in *Sudden Fiction International*. Robert Shapard & James Thomas, eds.  New York: W.W. Norton, 1989: 286–288.

Hutcheon, Linda.  *A Poetics of Postmodernism: History, Theory, Fiction.*  New York and London: Routledge, 1988.

Jameson, Fredric.  *Postmodernism, or, The Cultural Logic of Late Capitalism.*  Durham: Duke University Press, 1991.

Joyce, James.  *A Portrait of the Artist as a Young Man* in *The Portable James Joyce*.  New York: Viking Press, 1966: 243–526.

Kaplan, E. Ann. "Introduction," *Postmodernism and Its Discontents: Theories, Practices.* London-New York: Verso, 1988: 1–9.

Lyotard, Jean-François. *The Postmodern Condition: A Report on Knowledge.* Trans. Geoff Bennington and Brian Massumi. Minneapolis: University of Minnesota Press, 1984.

Martin, Stephen-Paul. "Gallery." *The Literary Review* 3,4 (Summer 1990): 450–451.

McHale, Brian. *Postmodernist Fiction.* New York: Methuen, 1987.

Nash, Christopher. *World-Games: The Tradition of Anti-Realist Revolt.* New York: Methuen: 1987.

# 6

# Man Has Fallen and He Can't Get Up: An Essay on Postmodernism and Advertising

*Roger Koppl*

## INTRODUCTION: YOU AIN'T HEARD NOTHIN' YET

Advertising is widely thought to be a bad thing. Beer-drinking dogs and bikini-clad hucksters come a long way short of Caravaggio or Grünewald or Frank Lloyd Wright. But advertising can be defended for the good it does. All things considered, even bad advertising promotes the social good. Bimbos wiggling across the TV screen do not cultivate the higher faculties. Hardly. But we live in an imperfect world. In particular, we cannot hope for any very radical improvement in human nature. So the good done by idiot ads only looks good in light of our shared human frailty.

Humans tend to seek salvation in various earthly pursuits. We become religious zealots committed to the pursuit of redemption. But we often seek this redemption through politics, food, sex, wealth, or something else short of communion with the divine. College professors sometimes place their hopes for salvation in a crackpot theory nobody else cares about. (The fools! They don't understand.) The search for earthly salvation can lead to bad things like holy wars, final solutions, and terrorist bombings. People act on their values. If they value most what they should not value at all, their actions may be trouble for the rest of us.

The good that advertising does may be seen in the light of this human tendency to seek out earthly salvation. The diversions created by stupid advertising focus different people's messianic impulses in different directions and on relatively unimportant things. That is the good they do. We seek redemption for our suffering through the new popularity we may enjoy if our teeth are baking-soda clean and our breath is minty fresh. We seek salvation in the new Mercedes Benz rag-top automobile. When these products disappoint us, we may turn to Soloflex exercise machines and 1-900 party lines. The wise among us may know that earthly salvation cannot be had. But the rest of us are off to the shopping mall for

Macy's big one-day sale.  And that's fine.  For if we were not tempted in this way by pimping advertisements, we might end up acting on the same foolish dream of redemption to the detriment of ourselves and our fellow humanity.  But for the lure of consumerism we might seek redemption through ethnic cleansing or a holy war against infidels.

This argument is developed in the context of "postmodernism."  (PoMo, as the hipsters call it, is very sexy stuff these days.)  But it is really an old argument, or at least a new twist on an old argument.  Back around 1700 or so, the Italian philosopher Giovanni Vico argued that "avarice" led to "commerce."  Avarice is a "vice" and commerce a cause of "civil happiness," so there must be a God who makes this transformation of human lead into social gold (quoted in Hirschman 17).  The argument of this chapter is in line with Vico's way of thinking.  David Hume, living in Scotland a few decades later, put it well: It would be great if we could make everyone perfect, but we cannot.  Sensible governments try to do only things that are really possible.  Since we can sometimes get rid of one bad thing only by replacing it with some other bad thing, governments should forget about getting things perfect and just pick the lesser of two evils.[1]  Greed is not good, but we can get  some good out of her.

The next section reviews postmodernism and the postmodern critique of advertising.  The following section argues that the postmodern assumption that we ought to get "liberated" is a bad one.  The final section builds on the two previous sections to argue that advertising is good because of its tendency to diffuse our messianic impulses.

## POSTMODERNISM AND ADVERTISING: BROTHER, CAN YOU SPARE A RHYME?

### What Is PoMo: Once upon a Time in the West

"Postmodern" is the sort of word whose meaning changes from author to author.  Even though nobody really knows just what it means, there is something out there to talk about.  So we have to use the word even though it has a fluid meaning.  To get at the meaning of PoMo, we need to gird our loins for a little history.

In any civilization, there is a tension between rational thought and traditional ways.  The result of this push and pull is that the ways in which people do things— build temples, paint, farm, make war, make love, talk, dress, and so on—change under the influence of rational thought, but only slowly.  That is how it was in Europe too.  Then there was the Renaissance and the emergence of "modern" Europe.  With each passing century, tradition lost ground and rational thought gained.  During the French Revolution they even drove the priests out of Notre Dame and set up a Church of Reason.  As Europe became ever more modern, the ways people did things and the ways they thought about things both became more rational.[2]

By the end of the 19th century, reason and "progress" could seem triumphant. Who would argue with Newton? The steam engine? Flush toilets? Then came the 20th century and Big Trouble. First and foremost there was World War I. A big, nasty, horrible, and incredibly stupid war like that was not supposed to happen. Moreover, all those great machines of the 19th century turned on us to become superefficient killers. That was not supposed to happen either.

The "Great War" is not the only thing we got hit with in the 20th century. There were all those weird ideas in physics. With Albert Einstein, time became "relative," space became "curved," and the old Euclidean geometry became just one of many possible structures for the "space-time continuum." The quantum physics we got from Werner Heisenberg and others was even weirder. God, it seems, *did* play dice with the universe. Particles could be waves too and that was supposed to be OK. This stuff can really give you a headache.

As if the curved space of physics were not enough, Sigmund Freud showed us that the space between the ears is also curved in weird ways. His epigram for *The Interpretation of Dreams* was well chosen: "If I cannot bend the higher powers, I shall stir up hell."[3] And it was hell to think about sex the way Freud did.

We had trouble in politics too. The Holocaust happened in the one of the most civilized countries in the world. Fascism and National Socialism were popular ideas. Many people pinned some high hopes on the Bolshevik Revolution in Russia. Unfortunately, Soviet leaders turned out to be a rather unsavory group, Joseph Stalin especially. Some folks would even say that the whole idea of rationally ordering economic affairs through central planning was a mistake (see Vaughn).

The troubles of the 20th century are reflected in its art: abstract art, cubism, New York action painting, machines that destroy themselves, surrealism, pop art, op art, Andy Warhol, and prize-winning paintings made by monkeys. Dada art was a response to World War I. If we live in an irrational world, we will make irrational art. Surrealism came from Freud's psychoanalysis. Let's do art by tapping into the subconscious. And Warhol was pure hype, the perfect artist for 20th century America.

In one area after another, the 20th century seemed to bring us uncertainty, indeterminism, confusion, and crisis. Even in mathematics, certainty was lost. In 1931, Kurt Gödel proved a theorem that made the whole idea of a "rigorous" mathematical proof pretty fuzzy. If you lay out some really tight rules for what counts as a proof, Gödel showed, either you have left something out or you have contradicted yourself. You have left something out if your standards will not let you prove every true theorem. You have contradicted yourself if your standards let you prove some mathematical statement and its denial, that is, if it lets you prove $A$ and not-$A$. Gödel showed that the only way to avoid contradicting yourself is to leave something out. (In more mathish lingo: Any axiom system rich enough to generate the arithmetic of whole numbers is either incomplete or inconsistent.)

There were other troubles too. Back in the 1880s, Georg Cantor came up with two new kinds of number, the "transfinite cardinals" and "transfinite ordinals." The trouble came in the 20th century when it was shown that you could make any of three contradictory assumptions about an important "transfinite cardinal" and still have a consistent system. In other words, there was more than one system of mathematics and nothing more solid than personal preference could choose between them![4] (All this is discussed in Kline.)

All of this uncertainty was hard to take. In one field of cultural activity after another, we found out that we did not really know what we thought we knew. We found that ways of thinking held in high regard in the 19th century were not really true, though some of them were useful. Modern Europe started out thinking that knowledge shows us how things are. We ended up thinking that knowledge shows us only how we think about things. This can be very upsetting. Friedrich Nietzsche saw it all coming and went insane. (Tertiary syphilis may have had something to do with this as well.)

By, say, 1970, we had been through a lot. Modernism had pretty much fallen apart. Interestingly, though, the wheels of commerce kept spinning as if there were nothing to worry about and nothing the matter. Regular folks went about their daily lives as if there were no culture crises to contend with. That was when people started to talk about postmodernism. The modernist project came crashing down on our heads and nobody noticed. Welcome to postmodernism.

Now, at last, a definition of "postmodernism" can be offered. (Do not take the definition too seriously. After all, nobody really knows what postmodernism is.) Postmodernism is everything we think, do, and say after the intellectuals have gotten it through their heads that modernism has come unraveled.

To make sense of postmodernism and its characteristic features, we had better distinguish between postmodernism as cultural moment and postmodernism as cultural critique. The postmodern cultural moment is what is going on around us even among people who never heard of postmodernism or, for that matter, modernism. The kinds of TV ads we get and the types of feeling people have when they see those ads are elements of the postmodern cultural moment. Writings about the postmodern cultural moment may be postmodern cultural criticisms, especially if they use words like "disjunctive," "decentered," and "layering."

The most evident feature of postmodernism as cultural moment is its mixing up of different styles in art and architecture. Postmodern cultural products use lots of different styles from the past. And they often show little concern for how these styles fit together. No style is better than the others, so why not mix them all up? The thought that one might make one's own style is modern, not postmodern. The thought that one might strive for a "true" or "pure" style is more than modern to the PoMo sensibility. It's a real knee-slapper.

The mixing of styles is a reflection of the second feature of PoMo life. It is sardonic. I know you are a faker and you know I am a faker and surely neither one of us has any sense of direction, let alone a mission or calling. But if you buy my painting, I will read your book, and neither one of us will have to face up to our own spiritual emptiness. We can carry on mixing styles to our hearts' content, or at least until the music stops and the party's over.

When sardonically mixing styles, it does not pay to have scruples about what is higher and lower, better and worse. Thus, the third feature of postmodernism is its fusing of high and low culture. The Pink Panther may show up on the television screen Saturday morning and the art museum Saturday afternoon.

If PoMo is the sardonic mixing of high and low styles, then it must be a sort of game. Mostly what goes on in today's centers of culture is gamesmanship. It may remind one of Hermann Hesse's *Glass Bead Game*. The Glass Bead Game, Hesse explains, is "a mode of playing with the total contents and values of our culture; it plays with them as, say, in the great age of the arts a painter might have played with the colors on his palette" (15). As for the rules, "[C]hanges in their number and order, and attempts at perfecting them, are actually no longer feasible except in theory" (15). The biggest difference between PoMo and the Glass Bead Game is this: The Glass Bead Game was "capable of expressing and establishing interrelationships between the content and conclusions of nearly all scholarly disciplines" (15). It was serious. It had some content. In the postmodern cultural moment, we do not believe, as did Hesse's players, that the games we play have any value. We play the game because that is the game and that is how you get ahead and we cannot imagine doing something really new and improved. Hesse believed; we do not.

Playing the postmodern game creates feelings of exhaustion and blankness; it levels and numbs. Postmodernism is the hegemonic rise of mediocracy. It's a drag. The trouble, postmodern types believe, is that we have tried everything else and run out of options.

### PoMo and Advertising: It Don't Mean a Thing, But It Still Got That Swing. Do-wop, Do-wop, Do-wop, Do-wop, Dada.

Postmodernism represents a kind of crisis. Postmodern cultural critique often tries to pin the blame for this crisis on "capitalism" or, perhaps, "late capitalism." Advertising is a capitalist activity *par excellence*. Thus, advertising-bashing has a secure place in the domain of postmodern cultural criticism.

Postmodern cultural critique can be hard to understand. The critics say things like this: In the postmodernist world, "The effluence of simulacra replaces the play of textuality or discourses in a universe with no stable structures" (Best & Kellner 121). Indeed. Luckily we need only get a feel for the postmodern critique of advertising. We can safely ignore problems of the effluence of simulacra and their ilk.

The essence of the PoMo critique of advertising is that advertising pimps. And, according to the PoMo critique, it is in the nature of capitalist advertising technique to attempt to ensnare us in a world of false hopes and shallow consumerism. The "hyped-up surface" of advertising carries us away from logic and "linearity" into a "pastiche" of false promises implied by absurd images of impossible salvations.  Humphrey Bogart, James Cagney, and Louis Armstrong, like the brothers Lazarus, have become posthumous pitchmen.  Driving the latest Jaguar is also, in some mysterious way, driving the classic cars of the past.  And the song accompanying the pictures implies that the Jaguar driving experience will be, somehow, the very joy of finding one's true love.  "Game Boy causes hipness" is a decidedly false advertising claim, and no one ever *said* it.  But the idea is conveyed perfectly well when we see a multicolored pastiche of hipness, hipsters, and hip happenings dancing madly about the modest electronic toy.

The postmodern critique of advertising, then, sees lies, lies, lies at every turn. What is more, the argument goes, the lies exploit our deepest and most nostalgic longings by promising a kind of earthly salvation in the American Dream of commodity fetishism.  (This chapter makes no attempt to decide if this criticism is valid.[5])

## IN DEFENSE OF ADVERTISING: PRIVATE VICES, PUBLICK VIRTUES, OR VISINE GETS THE GNOSIS OUT

### On Our Loss of Faith: God Is Dead, Long Live the King (Elvis, That Is)

The postmodern malaise is bred of a loss of faith.  As Todd Gitlin has pointed out, modernism, "whatever its subversive practices, [was] a series of declarations of faith—Suprematism's future, Joyce's present, Eliot's unsurpassable past" (360). All that has gone by the boards.  We are staring into the abyss and no place to leap. Even existential freedom is bogus when new forms of life and action no longer exist.  We have overdrawn our account at the bank of new salvations.

That is where advertising comes in.  We have turned our energies to the small-time salvation of shallow consumerism.  I'll buy tight buns from Jack Lalane, full lips from L'Oréal, and Ikea can give me the sort of furniture "real people" buy, and at discount prices too.  Drinking the right carbonated beverage will show that I'm not falling for that phony hipness stuff the way those people on the beach have.  All this will add up somehow to a fulfilled and successful life.  Especially successful. ("Americans," William James is supposed to have said, "worship the bitch goddess of success.")

The loss of faith and the retreat to consumerism would seem to make for a strong damnation of the capitalist system.  Surely we need to rescue postmodern man from the insidious clutches of late capitalism where his energies are siphoned off into the great sinkhole of consumerism?  Maybe not.

What advertising does is diffract the rays of our longing for salvation.  We have lost faith all right.  God is dead.  But we still long for some form of salvation.  We still seek some kind of liberation of the soul.  Advertising and consumerism give us outlets for this urge to salvation, outlets that point in different directions.  To see why this might not be such a bad thing, we need to look a little closer at both this human urge to salvation and some of its consequences.

**The Urge for Earthly Salvation: The Courage to Be a Shopper**

The urge to salvation runs deep in the human psyche. It is the wish—or need, if you like—to have faith in something. Not everyone feels it and not everyone who feels it reacts the same way to it. Nevertheless, it is a pretty strong impulse in many people. And plenty of people who feel it find something—Christ, Marx, or professional success—to have faith in.

Paul Tillich defines "faith" as "the state of being ultimately concerned" (1). That with which one is "ultimately concerned" is that in which one has faith. When you place your faith in something you get "the promise of ultimate fulfillment which is accepted in the act of faith" (2). If you believe, you interpret everything in the light of your faith. All your ideas about what is good and bad, trivial and important, all your judgments of value are shaped by your faith. Moreover, if you have faith, you are committed. "Faith," explains Tillich, "is definite in its direction and concrete in its content. Therefore, it claims truth and commitment. It is directed toward the unconditional, and appears in a concrete reality that demands and justifies such commitment" (40).

Many of us feel a kind of need for faith and hit upon things in which we have an "ultimate concern." Those of us who believe are committed because of our faith and we are waiting for the "ultimate fulfillment" promised by our faith. Ultimate fulfillment is a tall order. If you put your faith in the wrong object, you are sure to be disappointed. Misguided faith is called "idolatrous faith." "The inescapable consequence of idolatrous faith," Tillich warns us, "is 'existential disappointment,' a disappointment which penetrates into the very existence of man!" (40).

That is the trouble with the human urge toward salvation. Sometimes it leads people into idolatrous faiths that disappoint the believers at the deepest level.[6] And that can lead to trouble. National Socialism (Nazism) was a real faith for many good Germans. So too was Marxism for countless revolutionaries, Soviet bureaucrats, and Western college professors. Jim Jones created an idolatrous faith for his followers in Guyana. Nationalism has been an idolatrous faith in many times and places; it is something of an old standby in the idolatrous faiths department. Addicts have an ultimate concern with their drug.

As the examples of the last paragraph illustrate, the urge for faith and commitment can be dangerous. The real dangers come when you have a lot of people with the same misguided faith trying to do something about it. Lots of people going to church is fine even if their theological beliefs are mistaken. That is an otherworldly faith. The dangerous faiths are the ones that are earthly, widely held, and collective: Marxism, nationalism, supremacist racial doctrines, that sort of thing. These secular religions act like a lens to focus all the energies of the many believers on one object. But if they are, as I think they must be, idolatrous faiths, then the lens must be focused on the wrong object, and "existential disappointment" is sure to follow.

## How Advertising Diffuses Our Messianic Impulses: Just Buy It

The good that idiot advertising does is to disperse the energies of a thousand idolatrous faiths in a thousand different directions. It gives us a thousand points of disappointment. That is the good they do. That is why consumerism is not such a bad thing after all.

Idiot ads that insinuate false promises of ultimate fulfillment encourage people to place their faith in the products of commercial enterprise. We commit ourselves to white teeth and musk oil, hot cars and frozen foods. We do not commit ourselves to racial hatred, class conflict, nationalistic frenzy, or the glory of war.

In today's commercial society, advertisements offer us many false temptations. That sounds pretty bad. But the temptations of Madison Avenue do not threaten social harmony. If you put your faith in Calvin Klein, you will be disappointed. What will you do with your disappointment? Perhaps you will turn your heart's longing to Fendi or Gucci, saving up for that special suit or that one splendid pair of shoes. Perhaps you will learn a spot of wisdom, working a little more on your character, a little less on your wardrobe. In any event, the existential crisis caused by the failure of cool jeans to save your soul affects only you. The very day it hits, the rest of us are packing off to the mall for some more shallow consumerism. You will not march off to find the final solution, or kill the infidel, or ferret out anti-American teachers in our public schools.

What if you sought your earthly salvation in politics or social transformation or cultural identity? When disappointment strikes, you may learn wisdom. But you may instead learn to be more firm in your convictions, harder in your judgment of the wicked persons who do not see the political or social or cultural truth that you live for, quicker to take up arms, to act, to do *something* to change things radically from their current, putatively unacceptable state. Where once you saw disagreement, choices, and experiments in living, now you see yourself surrounded by wickedness and betrayal. Whatever other demerits such hardened attitudes to political and social questions may have, there is this: The very persons who have come to have such violent opinions cannot agree amongst themselves. Thus, bloodshed, suffering, and social disorder may follow.

Something of this dynamic, one might argue, is being played out in much of Eastern Europe, where the legacy of the old order seems to be "ethnic cleansing" and lots of bloodletting. We should prefer a world in which the earthly search for salvation has many little outlets. We should prefer a world in which the existential disappointments Tillich warned us of are private affairs and not public disasters. Commercial society—consumerism and all—provides us just such a world.

## CONCLUSION: ABADA-ABADA THAT'S ALL FOLKS!

The world would be a better place if no one were to put his faith in any earthly object.  Perhaps it would be better still if even the otherworldly faiths were abandoned.  But the fact is that people do still commit themselves to all sorts of foolish faiths.  The urge to find salvation in earthly pursuits is a bad thing, but no less real for all that.  Well then, let's try to minimize the harm of this bad thing.  By abiding the idiocies of a commercial society (if idiocies they be), we can let the messianic impulses of the urge to salvation, the destructive potential of idolatrous faith, be scattered in many different directions.  These energies are diffracted by the prism of market trading.  And that is better than letting them be focused by the lens of ideological passion.

## NOTES

1.  Hume put it this way: "Whatever may be the consequence of such a miraculous transformation of mankind as would endow them with every species of virtue and, and free them from every species of vice; this concerns not the magistrate who aims only at possibilities.  Very often he can only cure one vice by another; and in that case, he ought to prefer what is least pernicious to society" (31–32).

2.  This view of modernism owes plenty to the sociology of Max Weber.  For an introduction see Cohen.

3.  This is from Virgil's *Aeneid*.  In Latin: *Flectere si nequeo superos.  Acheronta movebo* (Schorske 200).

4.  What was shown was that the "cardinality" of the set of all subsets of the rational numbers could be assumed less than, equal to, or greater than the cardinality of the real numbers.  Any one of the three assumptions contradicts any other.  One must wonder, then, what it means to speak of the "cardinality" of the reals.

5.  In advertising, a considerable fraction of what is done is stupid, deceitful, and otherwise bad.  But the same may be said of any other human activity.  At least Madison Avenue is more diverting than Pennsylvania Avenue.  Or Sesame Street for that matter.

6.  It may not be completely unreasonable to wonder if all faith is ipso facto idolatrous.

## WORKS CITED

Best, Steven, and Douglas Kellner. *Postmodern Theory: Critical Interrogations*. New York: Guilford Press, 1991.

Cohen, Ira J. "Introduction to the Transaction Edition," *General Economic History*, by Max Weber. New Brunswick, N.J.: Transaction Books, 1981.

Cross, Mary. "Reading Television Texts: The Postmodern Language of Advertising," in this volume.

Gitlin, Todd. "Postmodernism: Roots and Politics," *Cultural Politics in Contemporary America*. Ed. Ian Angus and Sut Jhally. New York: Routledge, 1989.

Hess, Hermann. *The Glass Bead Game*. Trans. Richard Winston and Clara Winston. New York: Holt, Rinehart and Winston, 1969.

Hirschman, Albert O. *The Passions and the Interests: Political Arguments for Capitalism Before Its Triumph.* Princeton: Princeton University Press, 1977.

Hume, David. "Of Refinement in the Arts," in Hume, David. *Writings on Economics,* edited by E. Rotwein. Madison, Wisconsin: University of Wisconsin Press, 1970: 19–32.

Kline, Morris. *Mathematics: The Loss of Certainty.* New York: Oxford University Press, 1980.

Schorske, Carl E. *Fin-de-Siècle Vienna: Politics and Culture.* New York: Vantage Books, 1981.

Tillich, Paul. *Dynamics of Faith.* New York: Harper & Row, 1957.

Vaughn, Karen. "The Socialist Calculation Debate," in *The Elgar Companion to Austrian Economics.* Ed. Peter J. Boettke. Brookfield, Vt.: Edward Elgar, 1994: 478–84.

# 7

## Burroughs and Advertising: Fractured Language, Fractured Time, Fractured Image as the Universal Language

### *Michael B. Goodman*

In the late 1950s and early 1960s, William S. Burroughs' novels assaulted traditional narrative in fiction. Burroughs used several methods, among them "cut-ups." It was his attempt to create in linear form the same revolution that had almost a half century before transformed the world of painting and sculpture.

The result: "a frozen moment when everyone sees what is on the end of every fork." Burroughs was certainly not the first writer to push the limits of narrative; in fact, such efforts characterize much of 20th-century fiction and poetry. But his experiments with words and images captured and used fundamental changes in communication patterns brought on by movies, radio, and TV to tell a new type of story to a new type of audience. And, we might say, Burroughs' approach laid the foundation for the direction contemporary advertising was to take in its arrangement of words and images to replace narrative. The impact on the audience was visceral rather than intellectual.

Using TV as its vehicle, advertising has used the power of word and image to create a universal language. This essay explores the connections between Burroughs and advertising.

### NARRATIVE MEETS ELECTRONIC MEDIA

Burroughs has everything to do with advertising. And he pushed print into the visual media idiom long before most people had realized that electronic media would take over the world. Works after *Naked Lunch*—particularly *The Soft Machine* and *The Ticket That Exploded*—used his experiments with cut-ups to push the two dimensions of the page and the linearity of reading through to the simultanity of movies and television.

But it was *Naked Lunch* that started it all, a book so different in the changing postwar world of the 1950s that it created a censorship controversy much like the appearance of James Joyce's *Ulysses* in the 1920s. It was that generation's cause celebre.  And now Burroughs at 80 makes the bridge to the next generation as GenX-ers, reared on MTV, recognize in Burroughs a familiar visual idiom of juxtapositions and abrupt shifts.  It might also be his subject matter—sex, drugs, rock and roll—that attracts, but then almost everyone else has taken on these topics in fiction.  It is more likely the way Burroughs did it—matter of fact, with  a dash of black humor, a staring down and laughing  at the sorry  state of our cultural  landscape.

The universal appeal of rebellion has kept Burroughs fresh for every generation.  His anti-government stance, and his libertarian approach to free expression have attracted the literary community enough to tolerate his eccentricities.  He tapped into the forces that are changing our culture; the avant-garde has always been able to do just that, and Burroughs tapped the right ones for the American culture.

Events in Burroughs' life became the content of his art, connected by theme, but not in chronological sequence.  Guns, shootings, Mexico, dreams, drugs are all transformed in Burroughs' fiction (after all it was Burroughs who said that "history is fiction").  He showed through his novels, and the spare words and images of drugs and sex, the culture that was being fed to Americans at the end of that long newspaper spoon.  And, he discovered, breaking the order of narrative liberated both writer and audience to experience the events on many levels simultaneously.

## APPROACH AND METHODS THROUGH WORD AND IMAGE PATTERNS

What Burroughs was doing for novels was what early 20th century Russian film pioneer Sergi Eisenstein did for film.  Burroughs created a montage of images cut up and rearranged so that we get a new set of connections, a leap of intellect, a sort of black epiphany or humorous connection when none should have existed.

A train roar through him whistle blowing . . . boat whistle, foghorn, sky rocket burst over oily lagoon . . . penny arcade open into a maze of dirty pictures . . . ceremonial cannon boom in the harbor . . . a scream shoots down a white hospital corridor . . . out along a wide dusty street between palm trees, whistles out across the desert like a bullet (vulture wings husk in the dry air), a thousand boys come at once in outhouses, bleak public school toilets, attics, basements, treehouses, Ferris wheels, deserted houses, limestone caves, rowboats, garages, barns, rubbly windy city outskirts behind mud walls. (*Naked Lunch* 94–95)

Now digital video in movies like *Forrest Gump*, with its electronic pasting of actor Tom Hanks into historical footage such as that with President Kennedy or Lyndon Johnson or Martin Luther King, is an example of the kind of tricks and jokes Burroughs has been playing in all of his novels, and even his first "routine," "Roosevelt After Inauguration" (developed in the 1950s for friends Jack Kerouac and Allen Ginsberg, but not published until 1979).  He would get high with his friends and do these black comedy routines.  It was all very visual, all parody, all set with people in caricature, and all very useful in saying a great deal with very few words.  Of course, that is the artistic goal of good advertising—to say as much as possible with as little as possible; to meet those in the audience on many levels and make them remember and act.

Burroughs developed "cut-ups" to liberate images.  Advertising now does the same thing almost routinely to capture an audience's attention in a world of clutter and noise, compressing an enormous amount of information into a 30-second commercial.  It also liberates ideas through connections that may be hidden, unrevealed, or even suppressed.  Almost any commercial on MTV—or now on the major networks, for that matter—illustrates the code of juxtaposition and abrupt image shifts.  Burroughs himself explains that the cut-up method of writing was designed to "rub out the word" and "introduce the unpredictable spontaneous factor" into writing:

Cut the Word Lines with scissors or switch blade as preferred The Word Lines keep you in Time..Cut the in line..Make out lines to Space. Take a page of your own writing of you write or a letter or a newspaper article or a page or less or more of any writer living and or dead..Cut into sections. Down the middle. And cross the sides..Rearrange the sections.. Write the result message. (*The Exterminator* 5)

Sometimes the voice that results is prophetic and poetic, but most often it is just gibberish.  But Burroughs felt that cut-ups introduced a spontaneous, random factor freeing it from static linguistic combinations and associations.  Like the word paintings and  pastiche of advertising that Stuart Davis was  producing at the same time in the 50s (frontispiece).  Burroughs' word play defamiliarized the word, reinstating it as image.

He also developed an extension of the cut-up technique he called the fold-in method, which he said was designed to extend the limits of choice open to the writer.  At the 1962 Writers' Conference in Edinburgh, he explained the new method to an audience of writers including Norman Mailer, Mary McCarthy, Stephen Spender, Colin McInnes, and David Daiches: "A page of my text, my own or someone else's is folded down the middle and placed on another page.  The composite text is then read across, half one text and half the other" (*Edinburgh* 18). Of course, he noted that the process was not as random as one might think.  The selection of pages of similar topics gave better results, and some writers might see the technique more useful than would others.  He also explained that the technique was similar to flashbacks in a film and noted that the same methods had been used in music and film for years.

## IMPACT ON AUDIENCES—GUT, NOT INTELLECT

Audiences used to narrative and linear forms in novels were now exposed to Burroughs' efforts to inject the immediacy of the plastic arts of photography and painting and the simultaneity of film and music into the linear form of writing.  It is not surprising that during the same period Burroughs made several experimental films with Anthony Balch while in England, *The Cut-Ups* (1960, 1963, 1968) and *Towers Open Fire* (1993).

But how can we say Burroughs had an impact on advertising? It seems more than mere speculation to say that as an integral part of the avant garde art scene, Burroughs was influential on commercial advertising, which often tries to follow close behind artistic innovation. Advertising's creative and administrative centers, up until the early 1990s, were in New York City and London. Burroughs lived and worked as a writer in both until he moved to Lawrence, Kansas, in the 1980s. And when Burroughs entered the New York literary scene in the 1970s, he was presented as the legendary mentor of Kerouac and Ginsberg. He was, as the February 1974 issue of *Rolling Stone* described him, the Beat Godfather (24-27).

With a little help from his new literary agent, James Grauerholz, Burroughs began to go more mainstream. He was featured in New York at the Nova Convention (November 30 - December 2, 1978), produced in association with Grauerholz, John Giorno, Sylvere Lotringer, Entermedia Theatre, the Department of French and Italian at New York University, and the literary journal *Semiotext(e)*. The three-day event featured rock singer Laurie Anderson; a dialogue between Merce Cunningham and John Cage; and poetry readings by Anne Waldman, Ed Sanders, and Ginsberg. A panel included Timothy Leary and Susan Sontag. Films were shown, including these related to Burroughs: *Towers Open Fire* and *Cut-Ups*, Marc Olmstead's *Burroughs* (1977), and Steven Lowe's *Burroughs: Home Movies* (1976-1977). Performances included "A.J's Annual Party" from the play *Naked Lunch* adapted and directed by Donald Sanders; Philip Glass on the electric organ; Keith Richards; Patti Smith; and readings by Burroughs himself.

"Avant-Garde Unites Over Burroughs," shouted the *New York Times* that December, as the *Village Voice* exclaimed: "Why Is This Man Smiling? Thousands Cheer Burroughs at the Nova Convention." As if that were not mainstream enough for Burroughs, he appeared on "Saturday Night Live" in 1981, reading from his works.

Ultimately in 1992 David Cronenberg wrote and directed the movie *Naked Lunch* based on Burroughs' book. Peter Weller of *RoboCop*, Judy Davis, and Roy Scheider starred. The images Burroughs had written finally came to the big screen.

He had entered the mainstream decades before in a *Life* magazine article on the Beat movement, a scathing dismissal of almost everyone mentioned, but a soft recognition that Burroughs might, as an exception, be on to something. (O'Neill, 124-25.) That introduction certainly had no impact on advertising in the late 1950s, but his ideas of word and image seem to permeate almost any contemporary ad.

## UNIVERSAL IMPACT THROUGH IMAGE AND WORD

Advertising depends on a reaction.  Nike used Burroughs himself as an actor in its fall 1994 campaign.  He was not identified, of course, and the reaction from the *Village Voice* was uncertain.  Had Burroughs finally sold out?  Or was it the ultimate goof on corporate America?

Either way it is excellent advertising.  The image of Burroughs reading in his disembodied voice, clad in a business suit and hat, in his 80s certainly made a contrast to the jocks running, leaping, jumping across the TV screen ten or fifteen cuts per second in a blur.

Burroughs' connection to advertising and image making goes way back.  His mother's brother was Ivy Ledbetter Lee (1877-1934), who some consider the father of modern public relations.  Lee's use of "image" in his public relations work for John D. Rockefeller, Standard Oil, I.G. Farben, and other businessmen and corporations suggests a family connection upon which Burroughs developed his own very different and opposite ideas of "image" and "control."  "Lee" is a favorite pseudonym in his novels, a literary connection explored in Ted Morgan's excellent biography *Literary Outlaw: The Life and Times of William S. Burroughs* (1988). The impact of the industrial age and automation also has a family connection. Burroughs' paternal grandfather, William Seward Burroughs (1855-1898), was an inventor and model maker like his own father.  He is best remembered for his inventions and patents for machines that solved arithmetical problems.

Ads are really an American expertise.  Burroughs' voice taps into the root of the American voice.  He is always aware of his roots in literature.  He is never far away from the wry sarcasm of the carnival barker, which he shares with fellow Missouri writer Mark Twain and fellow St. Louis native T.S. Eliot.  Like them, he speaks the American idiom and taps into the black humor just beneath the surface of any true American tale.  In the ironies and inversions of a Burroughs novel, the knowing voice of the con man and artist guides us through a carnival of language that the marketplace was to recognize and appropriate for its own.

## WORKS CITED

"Avant-Garde Unites over Burroughs," *New York Times* 1 Dec. 1978: C11.

"Beat Godfather Meets Glitter Mainman: William Burroughs, Say Hello to David Bowie," *Rolling Stone* 155 (28 Feb. 1974): 24–27.

Burroughs, William S. "The Cut-up Method of Brion Gysin," *Yugen* 9 (1962): 31–35.

———. *Edinburgh Conference Proceedings*, 24 Aug. 1962: 18.

———. *Junkie.* New York: Ace, 1953.

———. *Naked Lunch.* New York: Grove Press, 1959.

Burroughs, William S. and Brion Gysin. *The Exterminator.* San Francisco: Hazelwood Books, 1960.

Cohen, Robert. "Dispatches from the Interzone." *New York Times Book Review* 15 Jan. 1995: 9.

Morgan, Ted. *Literary Outlaw: The Life and Times of William S. Burroughs*. New York: Henry Holt, 1988.

O'Neill, Paul. "The Only Rebellion Around," *Life* 47 (30 Nov. 1959):124-25.

"Why Is This Man Smiling?: Thousands Cheer Burroughs at the Nova Convention," *Village Voice* 11 Dec. 1978: 1+.

# 8

# The Selling of Gender Identity

## Judith Waters and George Ellis

There is good news and there is bad news. The good news is that print advertisements and television commercials have finally begun to respond to the needs
of a culturally diverse population. The bad news is that despite some progress, the
stereotyping of many groups based on gender, age, and race continues and leads
to some serious consequences. All too frequently women are still portrayed as sex
objects and in subservient roles. Sometimes, however, in an effort to target
segmented markets, we see some strange attempts at depicting egalitarianism. For
example, cigarette ads are now directed specifically toward working women
("You've come a long way baby"—now you, too, can die of lung cancer at the
same rate as men).

### THE IMPACT OF ADVERTISING

Advertising clearly plays a critical role in both reflecting and shaping culture.
Thus, while commercials and advertisements usually depict recognizable and
socially acceptable scenarios, they also attempt to mold public opinion with respect
to new products and services that people may not even know they want. What men
and women do know, what they have learned, are role-appropriate behaviors (e.g.,
the attributes or activities that contribute to the image of a successful male
executive or a good mother). The media reinforce these concepts. They try to
convince women that one of their major responsibilities is to remain magically
young and attractive forever by purchasing the correct products and services.

For example, in the June 1995 issue of *Vogue* magazine, a whole periodical
devoted to appearance, fashion, health, and other women's issues, a Revlon
advertisement for Age Defying Makeup shows Melanie Griffith (a near-forty film
star) with copy that talks about how to look younger. While most manufacturers are
very careful not to promise miracles, if the reader is not careful the message starts

to sound as if real changes in the texture of the aging skin will occur. This product says only that it makes fine lines seem to disappear. "Seem" is the operative word.

Further on in the same magazine, Estée Lauder, another cosmetic company, promotes Advanced Night Repair: Protective Recovery Complex. This company claims that the product will prevent environmental damage from ultraviolet rays and free radicals that may cause premature aging (a condition clearly to be avoided at all costs). Another ad by Lancôme describes a product called Expressive which should be used to reinforce the fragile eye area. Among the articles in the same issue of *Vogue* are "Reversing Sun Damage" and "Perfecting the Fake Tan," a way of looking tanned without incurring the skin damage that results from natural tanning. The preponderance of information and ads on skin care in women's magazines clearly plays on their fears of aging and abandonment.

Lest one think that advertisers have ignored the vanity of the male reader, in the March 1995 issue of *GQ* (*Gentlemen's Quarterly*), there is an ad for Clinique's Face Scrub, part of its line of skin supplies for men. The ad says the product will revive a man's looks. The balance of advertisements and articles in a magazine that targets a male readership, however, differs from that found in such periodicals as *Vogue, Harper's Bazaar, Cosmopolitan, and Seventeen.* Most of the ads in *GQ* are for clothing, shoes, alcoholic beverages, and cars (sometimes in two-page spreads). The only other appearance-related ad is for Rogaine, to regrow hair. The ad describes research results, complete with statistics, to demonstrate Rogaine's effectiveness. This issue of *GQ* contains no major articles on skin care and only a few on exercise. The rest focus on selling expensive clothing items. Very few women are depicted in either the articles or the ads. When they are shown, they are usually completely nude. In a Calvin Klein ad for his men's cologne, Obsession, Kate Moss, an almost childlike model, reclines nude and alone looking straight at the camera. The inference is clearly that someone similar to her will be waiting for the user of Obsession.

There is nothing new about the focus on eternal youth and beauty. For years, cosmetic and skin care products have been sold to women with the promise of looking younger and/or catching a man. The slogan for Pond's cold cream linked it with being engaged. A recent Maybelline commercial suggests that the female models look younger than they are because they use its products. What a miraculous process, ten years off your life instantly. The men's skin care market never really grew as many experts predicted it would. In the last few years, ads and commercials have played not only on male sexual anxieties, but also on the fear of losing one's job to younger competitors. Advertisers are very adept at addressing every group's insecurities and survival and self esteem needs.

## SEGMENTING

Both the female and the male markets are segmented by age, ethnic and racial group, socioeconomic class, urban or rural environment, occupation, and marital status.  The interactions among these categories further divide both markets.  Thus, the needs and wants of a twenty-something African-American single mother who has a full-time job and lives in an urban environment have been recognized as being different from those of men and women in other categories.  Magazines such as *Ebony* and *Essence* address these needs and  send messages about the values they support.

Since times change, evaluations of a segmented market's needs and wants must be constantly updated.  For example, the clothing preferences of women in their forties in the 1950s were very different from those of the same age category today.  Their discretionary buying power and their need to please other family members before themselves have also changed.  Women in this age category are more likely to be employed outside the home than they once were, to be divorced, to have little time for shopping and food preparation or even a strong interest in such activities.  Instead, "They  prize convenience and  service  when  they  shop" (Leeming & Tripp 103).

Survey  data  indicate  that  women  are  still  the  primary  shoppers  for  an overwhelming  majority  of  American  households.   It  is  estimated  that  the percentage ranges from 70 percent to 85 percent in terms of the purchase of groceries and durable goods.  Many social changes have influenced the impact of women not just as gatekeepers for the household, but also as individuals making their own choices.  Historically the needs of the country during World War II brought more women into the economy and placed them in decision-making positions.  After the war, with the advent of the women's movement and the development of effective birth control measures, even women who could do so were often unwilling to resume traditional roles.  With high divorce rates and economic problems, it became all the more imperative that women support themselves and their children. They developed new needs and wants.  Prepared foods and fast-food emporiums began to flourish.  Other lifestyle changes included putting a premium on efficient time utilization and labor- and time-saving devices.  Magazine spreads and ads for convenience products, clothes, and other important items that actually save the shopper time and effort appeared now.  TV networks and home shopping catalogues cater to the individual or family whose time constraints make shopping very difficult, if not impossible.  On the other hand, a visit to the local mall on the weekend seems to be a very popular pastime.

Many contemporary women, despite layoffs and recent economic downturns, have sufficient discretionary income to spend on the goods and services they want.  They  are  more  educated  and  sophisticated  than  previous  groups  of  female consumers. While the women's market is multidimensional, relating to both the demographics and the psychographics of each segment, there is a similarity in women's critiques of the content of advertising campaigns.  Not only do many of them find some of the content offensive, but also they suggest that women continue to be stereotyped (so are men) and that they cannot relate to the female models who are  very  young,  very  thin,  and  very  beautiful.   These  women  also  criticize infomercials as being extremely misleading.  Some of these infomercials use a very hard sell approach, sometimes bordering on fraud, to promote expensive skin products, special diet programs, and exercise equipment (also directed at men).

## GENDER IDENTITY AND THE USE OF STEREOTYPES

The advertiser constructs a scene complete with actors using scripts to send a message to a target audience. Due to the brevity of these mini plays, the message must be easily decodable, but not insulting to the audience's intelligence. Therefore, the use of recognizable models or stereotypes for the characters facilitates the advertiser's goal of selling products to specific groups. Audiences have become more sophisticated in recent years than they once were. For example, they may wonder if the film has been retouched or if the actors who are posing as normal and natural people are actually wearing concealing theatrical makeup.

Regardless of one's philosophical or political position on feminist issues, gender is still one of the most basic categories in any culture (Taylor, Peplau, & Sears 371). The process by which we identify not only people, but also vocabulary and speech patterns, gestures and behaviors, objects, and activities as either "masculine" or "feminine" is called "gender typing." Gender stereotypes are schemata (cognitive structures) about traits and behaviors that are perceived as typical of average or "normal" men and women. Sometimes an attribute that is positively correlated with one sex is seen as a negative or abnormal characteristic in the other, even among mental health professionals who should know better. While we can easily identify examples of cultural stereotypes that have more or less universal recognition within the society, many people hold personal stereotypes that deviate in one or more ways from those cultural images. Personal stereotypes are frequently based on individual experience. Cultural stereotypes strongly influence our perceptions of people, particularly when specific information is limited and when the issue of gender itself is salient. There is already sufficient evidence in the social sciences to indicate that stereotypes can bias the evaluation of the characteristics and performances of individuals and whole groups (e.g., women drivers). One of the most serious consequences of the influence of stereotypes is that as a member of a society, a person may actually accept its beliefs about masculinity and femininity and incorporate those beliefs as important elements in his or her own self-concept. If that person's traits and characteristics fail to meet the social ideal, the result is frequently low self esteem and sometimes even depression.

When we encounter new people for the first time, we engage in a process of person perception that depends on a quick interpretation of their attributes, especially the visible ones. Usually the process is automatic and surprisingly accurate. For example, when we meet a small child dressed in blue jeans, a white tee-shirt, and sneakers and sporting a short haircut, we assume the child is a little boy. If we discover we are wrong, we feel not only embarrassed, but probably cheated as well. Little girls are supposed to dress like girls even at play. The shirt should have been pink or printed with flowers. The hair should have been longer and tied with a ribbon. We have developed expectations that people should and will utilize appropriate dress and other cues to their gender identity. Most of the time they do.

Although we may decry the use of sex-role stereotypes (both positive and negative) as limiting, they do serve a purpose, or they would not survive (a little Social Darwinism). In this complex world, with its myriad conflicting inputs, we try to simplify our information-seeking and decision-making processes. Stereotypes help us to come to rapid conclusions, which, albeit incorrect in many instances, keep society moving. In these times of constant change and disconfirmed expectations, men and women alike would prefer to have the "right" answers, the correct way of behaving, and the most appropriate strategies for success handed to them on the proverbial silver platter. We look toward experts to provide simple and easily processed answers to our problems. Commercials appear to do just that; they give us the one-minute solution. Many of the products deal with some of our most pressing needs, such as the need to feel safe, secure, and loved as men and women. Despite the fact that we live in an age and a milieu of changed ideals and metaphors as well as altered family structures and evolving work and class relations, there is a nostalgia, a yearning for times that seem to have been simpler and more manageable. For example, contemporary brides frequently choose the most traditional gowns. Bridesmaids are dressed to look like shepherdesses in the middle of middle-class, middle America. The reality of the divorce rate, the predominance of female-headed households, and the growth of a huge underclass typified by urban poverty are only beginning to be reflected in the media.

While the focus of postmodernism has been on the philosophical aspects of social analysis, feminists have emphasized social criticism and have often attacked the contents of media programming and advertising. The critic Harold Bloom (cited in Lehman) proposed the title "The School of Resentment" as an umbrella term for the critical theories that he saw emanating from university literature departments. Among these theories, he included deconstructionists, semioticans, and the most recent school of feminists. He suggests that "literary criticism is used as a weapon on behalf of groups perceived as historical victim—it is their way to get even with their oppressors" (quoted in Lehman 27). The implication is that the criticism is more vindictive than it needs to be. However, if we go all the way back to G.W. Allport's *The Nature of Prejudice* and Erving Goffman's works on gender, we find that insufficient change has been been made in recent decades with respect to negative gender and racial stereotypes. The critiques are more than justified. Innovation in advertising seems to involve selling what we did not know we needed to solve problems we did not know we had in the service of some traditional and some new goals using creative and postmodernist strategies.

Goffman defines advertisements as "highly manipulated representations of recognizable scenes from 'real life.' " In her introduction to Goffman's book on gender in advertising, Vivian Gornick states that the feminists have prodded social scientists into examining the most ordinary exchanges and behaviors that involve men and women so that a better understanding of the social forces that account for these behaviors is developed. Goffman himself suggests that we ought to ask ourselves what ads tell us about ourselves. He also suggests that we should question the relationship between what we see as constructed images (ads and commercials) and so-called natural behavior.

In the scripted and manipulated commercial, however fanciful, the scene must strike a responsive chord and play to the audience's system of needs and values, or it will not sell products. Ads do not necessarily display how men and women actually behave, but how we think or wish they would behave. We suspend our disbelief in an effort to accept the storyline we are seeing. Otherwise, we would have to believe that the choice of a coffee or cereal brand occupies most of the waking thoughts of people in the real world.

The advertising industry has become so influential in educating people about how to behave and dress that it is being called upon to solve major social problems such as substance abuse and the transmission of AIDS. At the same time that the field is being asked to respond to social challenges, fashion models (both male and female) have become the new celebrities. In fact, teenage models who are not required to act or even talk have become the ideal of womanhood in magazines. "In the fashion world of the 90s," according to Jennifer Egan in a Sunday *New York Times Magazine* article, "teenage models simulate an adulthood they've yet to experience for women who crave a youthful beauty they'll never achieve" (26). The lifestyle of "James" King, a 16-year-old highly successful model, actually warranted the cover and 14 pages of the *Times* Sunday magazine. Many of these models are school dropouts who live on coffee and cigarettes to maintain their anorectic images. The worship of adolescent models has inspired many young (and older) women to follow their dieting regimen, with serious consequences.

The women in most ads that depict an upper-upper-class life style are thin, are well built (nudity is no problem), and engage in gazing at the successful males in their lives. They often have their fingers in their mouths or are touching their own hair. The implication is that they achieved their enviable status by attracting a male protector, not by earning the income themselves. In 1979, Goffman wrote that women are "being saved from seriousness" by posing and acting like children, lowering their eyes, and being seductive. Have times changed? We think not enough. Such roles and behaviors as Goffman discusses may be as stifling and constricting to men as to women. Most rigid, stereotyped, and asymmetrical role relationships constrain behavior on both sides. Some asymmetrical roles such as host and guest are dyadically reversible. Since the participants have the opportunity to play both parts at different times, they may not be troubled by the one-sidedness of temporary relationships. If, however, the asymmetrical relationship is relatively permanent and clearly has advantages associated with the dominant position and disadvantages associated with the subservient position, the lower-level participant may engage in ingratiation techniques, work hard at being lovable and attractive, or rebel.   For those who want to please, there are innumerable products to assist in the process.

## THE NATURE OF "REAL" MEN AND WOMEN

In the analysis of "signs" (indicators) about human behavior, Goffman wrote that "a particular behavior need not be construed as characteristic of a class of individuals but the *tendency* to possess such states and concerns is seen as an essential attribute" (7). A behavior may attract attention simply because it is *not* considered a natural component of the person's gender identity.  A man may be shown diapering a baby, but the act is not necessarily considered an essential expression of maleness, or a woman who works may be considered a marginal laborer who is only marking time until she can find a man to take care of her and can be a real woman.

The nature of gender-essential elements may differ according to the characteristics of the audience.  For example, women perceiving themselves as a group may identify different characteristics than men asked to delineate the basic nature of women.  Depending on the level of enculturation, there will, of course, be many similarities in both perspectives.  Accurate communication and consensus about the essential elements in gender identity becomes a function of well-learned rituals and symbols rather than spontaneous expressions.  Many individuals learn to simulate gender-appropriate behaviors successfully in order to gain or maintain membership in a particular reference group (e.g., heterosexual teenage males).  Due to the strong influence of socializing agencies including the media, an individual may manifest a behavior that appears to be" spontaneous and unselfconscious, that is uncalculated, unfaked, natural" (Goffman 7), but that may in actuality be contrived and constructed.  According to Goffman, "One might as well say there is no gender identity.  This is only a schedule for the portrayal of gender" (8).

Gender identity is not the only focus of the advertising industry.  Commercial pictures, moving and otherwise, have long been used to sell the image of a group of people.  In *The Faces of the Enemy,* Sam Keen  clearly delineates how nations have sold the justification for war and destruction by depicting the enemy with animal-like faces (e.g., pigs and snakes) so that killing them seemed a reasonable act.

## ANALYTIC CATEGORIES IN GENDER ADVERTISING

Goffman used a number of categories in his analysis of gender advertising that are equally relevant today.  They include relative size and position, the feminine touch, function ranking, and the  family.

**Relative Size**

Power, authority, rank, office, and renown are often depicted by relative size for both same-sex and opposite- sex relationships. In this world, of course, the average man *is* taller that the average women, but not necessarily so. In a study conducted by Judith Waters (unpublished data) a few years ago, college students were shown one of a set of three photographs of two young adults (a male and a female). In one photo, the man appeared taller than the woman, while in the second, they were both the same height, and in the third, the woman appeared taller. Students were asked to write brief stories about each "couple." Invariably they saw the photo of the taller man and shorter woman as a scene between lovers. On the other hand, the taller woman was described as a parent, a sister, a teacher, or an employer, but never as a romantic character. The couple of equal size were also described as relatives or just friends. If we watch commercials and TV dramas and comedies, we find few fictional or real-life couples where the woman appears taller. One exception to this rule is Jill Eikenberry and Michael Tucker, characters on the once popular "L.A. Law" and married in real life. In a study of children's readers from five countries, Florence L. Denmark and Judith Waters found that boys were usually represented as older and taller than their sisters, who were often shown sitting at their feet. In some recent ads in the *New York Times*, women have been seated childlike on the floor. If you look at the height of their heels and the flimsy support of the shoes, it is probable that they could not stand or walk anyway. Most women call this type of footgear "sitting shoes."

Ben Zion Chanowitz and Robert Hanlon conducted a study of the ideal height differential for a male and female couple and found that it was four inches (with the male being taller, of course) (cited in Denmark and Waters 10). The average American man is 5 feet 9 inches and the average American woman is 5 feet 6 inches. If the woman is wearing three-inch heels, there is definitely a problem. The male does not always have to be taller than the rest of the group. Goffman demonstrated that sometimes power is depicted by having the male seated while others such as family members stand around him.


**Feminine Touch**

The way that women use their hands (complete with professionally polished long nails) and touch themselves, children, animals, or men demonstrates that they are still perceived as the gentle and graceful sex. Women, especially young women, are also shown with a finger or fingers in their mouths, just to remind us how vulnerable and powerless they are and how much they are in need of protection.

**Function Ranking**

When Goffman published *Gender Advertisements* in 1979, he had ample evidence for status differentials in print ads, with numerous examples of women as nurses and secretaries often taking instruction from a wiser man. Recent commercials, however, targeted to the ever-growing population of working and professional women, do portray women in positions of responsibility. In a commercial for Saturn automobiles, a young female customer becomes so incensed at the sexist way an auto salesman deals with her that she decides to become a salesperson herself.

In advertising, voice-overs are more frequently male than female. The implication is that the male voice is more authoritative and credible even for household products than the female voice. Thus, it is clear that advertising conveys messages about the nature of men and women in both open and subtle ways. While in recent years there have been some changes, probably in order to avoid alienating potential customers, traditional stereotypes are still used extensively.

In their text, *Social Psychology*, Shelly E. Taylor, Letitia Anne Peplau, and David O. Sears summarize themes observed in the portrayal of men and women not only in advertising but in other publications such as children's literature in the following way:

Whereas men are shown in a wide variety of social roles and activities, women are more often restricted to domestic and family roles. Men are commonly portrayed as experts and leaders, women as subordinates. Men are usually depicted as more active, assertive, and influential than women. Although females are slightly more than half of the population, they are underrepresented in the media. (373)

## The Family

More diverse types of family structures are growing in popularity with advertisers. A recent MCI commercial shows a large extended-family reunion with a voice-over by a man who acknowledges he is divorced and living in a different state from his ex-wife and their children, which is the reason he needs MCI's "friends and family" telephone service. In an instant- coffee commercial that has developed into a sort of mini-series, the female lead (and romantic partner) is discovered to be divorced with an adult son. Although this scenario is a new way of depicting relationships, her physical appearance is still emphasized. The woman looks only about five years older than her fictional offspring.

## Sexuality in Advertising

In addition to Goffman's categories, we wish to suggest one of our own perspectives for evaluating the roles of men and women. This category is the relative use of men and women as blatant sex objects.  Calvin Klein, who sells his perfumes and colognes with both nude females and nude males, is actually very democratic.  This is rarely the case.  Advertisements for products in such women's magazines as *Cosmopolitan* depict men and women in romantic poses with the women in attractive and seductive outfits, while in *Gentlemen's Quarterly*, the women generally wear fewer clothes than the men, if anything at all.  In one recent ad, there is a full-page display of a completely naked model bent over a pool table supposedly playing pool, but clearly waiting to be sodomized.  There is no doubt that the advertisers are selling one image of women to women and another to the male audience.  While it is much more difficult to engage in that type of market segmentation on TV than it is in the print media, one has only to watch major sporting events to see a more sexual view of women than those presented on both daytime and nighttime "soap operas."  The emphasis on romance in *Cosmopolitan* and sex in *Gentlemen's Quarterly* is still the product of traditional stereotypes.

There is further evidence for variability in the quality of male and female images in the media.  In a content analysis of 2,209 network TV commercials selected from daytime, evening,  prime time, and weekend afternoon sports programming, R.S. Craig found that due to the imbalanced composition of the audience (e.g., more males than females watch sportscasts on Sunday afternoon), stereotypes matched the nature of the target market's image.  Women in daytime programs are generally shown as American housewives and in subservient roles, while they are depicted as sex objects during sportscasts.  However, commercials in evening programs other than sportscasts generally portray women in a more egalitarian and sophisticated fashion.

The correlation between the use of specific stereotypes on TV and the nature of the audience is not clearly causal.  We must question whether TV programming and commercials, especially during daytime hours, encourage traditional sex-role behavior or whether traditionalists watch more TV because the content reinforces their preexisting beliefs.  The answer is probably a little bit of column A and a little bit of column B.

## THE PERVASIVENESS OF MEDIA INFLUENCE

In a study of the impact of TV commercials on participant behaviors, Jennings, Geis, and Brown found that whether or not consumers actually purchase the products advertised, they may be influenced by the implicit gender-typed messages that the commercials send.  Clearly, of course, although not everyone personally accepts cultural stereotypes, these stereotypes still affect how people are treated and the jobs for which they will be hired.  People discriminate even when they are not prejudiced.  Since D.J. Bergen and J.E. Williams found that stereotypes about the personal characteristics of men and women have remained surprisingly stable over the years, these problems are likely to continue.

Segmenting markets does not alter the trend toward stereotyping. While there are stereotypes that pertain to men and women in general, there are specific stereotypes for different categories of men and women (e.g., mothers, grandmothers, teachers, librarians, corporate career women, teenage babysitters, and actresses). For example, people are very surprised to find that an actress or model has an advanced degree such as a Ph.D. We form schemata about specific categories of men and women that include personality traits, physical appearance, mode of dress, intellectual capacity, and typical behavior. Some of these schemata may even contain a grain of truth. The problem, however, is that it is very difficult to know whether the individuals in any single category naturally possess these traits or simply attempt to live up to their stereotypes.

It should come as no surprise that people respond more to the individual traits of a person and less to stereotypes when there is an opportunity to become better acquainted with the person. In advertisements, unless a well-known person (a celebrity, for example) is employed, the audience is supplied only with a brief scripted stereotype. With print ads, there is only a frozen image to use as a source of information. Limited information, as previously noted, increases the reliance on stereotyping.

## THE CONSEQUENCES

The issue of gender stereotyping in advertising may seem trivial compared to some of society's more serious problems. This is especially true when we are discussing fashion and cosmetics. However, stereotyping can actually have very negative consequences. One study of gender bias in medical advertising found that physicians may be influenced by how men and women "patients" are portrayed in the ads in medical journals. First of all, women continue to be underrepresented in the ads. Second, women tend to look younger than the men, which implies that older women are unimportant or non-existent. In addition, the men look "serious," according to the research participants, while the women look "pleasant." The inference is that women's symptoms are to be taken less seriously than men's. Since cardiovascular disease, as one example, is the primary cause of death in this country for both men and women, even subtle negative messages about the nature of women patients can be hazardous for their health. A casual examination of medical journals devoted to women (e.g., *The Female Patient*) indicates that a major category of advertisements is for psychotropic drugs such as Valium and Prozac. The implication may be that women's complaints are essentially psychological in origin, which precludes the necessity for laboratory testing or medical treatment.

The emphasis  on physical attractiveness and weight loss in women's magazines, especially those targeted toward adolescent or young adult readers, may also lead to negative consequences. The inferences  women draw from these advertisements are that one can never be too thin and that the end justifies the means. Thus, commercials or advertisements may cause or support the recent increase in such eating disorders as anorexia nervosa.

One of the most serious problems with the use of stereotypes on TV, whether in the scripts of programs or in commercials, is that children consume hours of TV messages each day. The more time children spend watching TV, the more they tend to hold stereotypic views of men and women and the jobs for which each sex is supposedly suited. Such children believe that only girls wash dishes and that only boys mow lawns and take out the garbage. They are also likely to retain these stereotypes as they grow older.

## SUMMARY

Research indicates that while some positive changes have occurred in the way that men and women are portrayed in advertisements and commercials, stereotypes that can result in damaging consequences to every member of the population still exist. Although these stereotypes are marketed differently depending on the composition of the audience, they are available not only to all adults, but also to impressionable children. As two pragmatic applied psychologists, we suggest that the best social action to take in order to change the situation may be to boycott products that are promoted with sexist advertising messages. Such "green" power has always worked.

## WORKS CITED

Allport, G.W. *The Nature of Prejudice.* Reading, Mass.: Addison-Wesley Publishing Company, 1954.

Anderson, A.E., and L. DiDomenico. "Diet vs. Shape Content of Popular Male and Female Magazines: A Dose-Response Relationship to the Incidence of Eating Disorders?" *International Journal of Eating Disorders* 11. 3 (1992): 283–87.

Bergen, D.J. and J.E. Williams. "Sex Stereotypes in the United States Revisited: 1972–1988." *Sex Roles* 24 (1991): 413–23.

Bretl, D.J., and J. Cantor. "The Portrayal of Men and Women in U.S. Television Commercials: A Recent Content Analysis and Trends Over 15 Years." *Sex Roles* 18 (1988): 595–609.

Caplan, P.J., and J.B. Caplan. *Thinking Critically About Research on Sex and Gender.* New York: Harper Collins, 1994.

Craig, R.S. "The Effect of Television Daytime Programs on Gender Portrayals in Television Commercials: A Content Analysis." *Sex Roles* 26 (5-6): 197-211.

Denmark, Florence.L., and Judith Waters. "Male and Female in Children's Readers: A Cross Cultural Analysis." *Basic Problems in Cross Cultural Psychology.* Ed. Y.H. Poortinga. Amsterdam and Lisse: Swets and Zeitlinger, B.V., 1978.

Durkin, K. "Sex Roles and the Mass Media." Ed.D.J. Hargreaves & A.M. Colley, *The Psychology of Sex Roles.* New York: Hemisphere, 1987. 201–14.

Eagan, Jennifer. "James is a Girl." *The New York Times Magazine* 4 Feb. 1996: 26-35+

Goffman, Erving. *Gender Advertisements.* New York: Harper & Row, 1979.

Jennings, J., F.L. Geis, and V. Brown. "Influence of Television Commercials on Women's Self Confidence and Independent Judgment." *Journal of Personality and Social Psychology* 39.2 (1980): 203–10.

Jung, C.G., and M.L. Von Franz. *Man and His Symbols.* Garden City, N.Y.: Doubleday & Co., Inc., 1971.

Keen, Sam. *The Faces of the Enemy: Reflections of the Hostile Imagination.* San Francisco: Harper & Row, 1986.

Kimball, M.M. "Television and Sex-Role Attitudes." *The Impact of Television: A Natural Experiment in Three Communities.* Ed. T.M. Williams. Orlando, Fla.: Academic Press, 1986. 265–301.

Kleppner, Otto, T. Russell, and G. Verrill. *Otto Kleppner's Advertising Procedure.* Englewood Cliffs, N.J.: Prentice Hall, 1983.

Lasch, Christopher. *The Culture of Narcissism.* New York: Warner Books, 1979.

Leeming, E.J., & C.E. Tripp. *Segmenting the Women's Market.* Chicago: Probus Publishing Company, 1994.

Lehman, David. *Signs of the Times: Deconstruction and the Fall of Paul de Man.* New York: Poseidon Press, 1991.

Leppard, Wanda, Shirley-Matile Ogletree, and Emily Wallen. "Gender Stereotyping in Medical Advertising: Much Ado about Something?" *Sex Roles* 29 (1993): 829-838.

Nicholas, L.J. *Feminism/Postmodernism.* New York: Routledge, 1990.

Signorelli, N., and M. Lears. "Children, Television, and Conceptions About Chores: Attitudes and Behaviors." *Sex Roles* 27 (1992): 157–70.

Taylor, S.E., L.A. Peplau, and D.O. Sears. *Social Psychology.* 8th ed. Englewood Cliffs, N.J.: Prentice Hall, 1994.

Wilkie, W.L. *Consumer Behavior.* New York: John Wiley & Sons, 1986.

# 9

# Advertising as Educator

## Donald W. Jugenheimer

Advertising can represent the worst of our culture and often does. At its worst, advertising mirrors the lowest depths of what we term our culture. At its median, advertising brings us kitsch culture. At this highest mark, advertising represents the breadth of our popular culture.

As a reflection of popular culture, advertising imitates the base elements of everyday life, duplicates the monotonous and bland, copies the dullest aspects that appear in the mass media as well as in everyday life

Yet advertising is not only a follower of weak trends and mediocre tastes. It can teach. It can provide useful information. It can actually enhance people's lives. Advertisers often consider whether they should simply follow the mood and taste of the public or should serve in a leadership role, exposing the public to new heights, presenting the average person with new tastes, encouraging those who are satisfied with the status quo to seek novelty, improvement, and enhancement.

Certainly advertising has brought much to popular culture and to culture in general. And, for better or for worse, advertising has served as role model, fashion model, even learning model. TV commercials are perhaps the most obvious and pervasive type of advertising in modern life. Commercial announcements are often intrusive, repetitive, loud, irritating, and obnoxious. Yet those same traits are among the factors that lend advertising its instructive mode.

Film buffs look back to a Beatles movie, *The Yellow Submarine*, as the forerunner of modem film-making techniques. That film introduced rapid cuts from one scene to another, fast movement that dominated the screen with non-violent action, and sound cuts that preceded the visual cuts—hearing the beginning of the next scene while the last scene was still being shown visually, a quick transition that kept the audience involved, attentive and interested. These factors may have been new to cinema, but they were hardly novel to advertising. Advertising on TV had for some time used these techniques of quick visual cuts, motion dominance, and sound transfer ahead of visual transfer.

In commercial announcements, these audience-involving approaches were used for purposes identical with the outcomes in the film: maintaining interest, attention, and involvement.

And TV had also adopted similar techniques from advertising production. Sports telecasts were among the initiators with this imitation: The Munich Olympics on the ABC television network had used fast cuts from one venue to another, intermixing sports images and locations.   Similarly golf telecasts had cut rapidly from one player and hole to another in order to step up the pace of this comparatively slow sport.

Advertising has brought more than production techniques to popular culture. Believe it or not, morality standards have also been a function of advertising, again with the specific case of TV commercials.   Advertising has not been as base or immoral as one might at first suspect.   The standard for many TV commercial producers, those who have produced announcements for products and services that appeal to sex and scatology, has been TV itself: The copywriters and producers have looked to daytime serial programs, what we know commonly as "soap operas," for their guidance as to what is acceptable and to what limits they can go with their commercials, particularly the visual aspects, but also the implied and alluded to.   In this particular role, advertising may serve as a follower, not a leader.

But advertising is at least reticent to break through to new depths and peeps, upholding morality by holding back, retaining standards by lagging in exposure and voyeurism.   To some, it may be a frightful omen that our media mores are established by "As the World Turns."

## LEARNING FROM ADVERTISING

Advertising has an even stronger role as instructor.   One of the precepts of learning theory is repetition to enhance learning and induce recall.   Obviously advertising uses repetition in its attempt to gain recognition, recall, knowledge, desire, preference and acquisition.   Indeed, one of the sins of advertising is that it overdoes the repetition.   On TV, repetition to the extreme leads to irritation on the part of the audience, perhaps even to rejection, what is termed in the advertising business as "the irritation factor."

So advertising makes use, intentionally or not, of learning models and theories. And as it is wont to do, advertising goes too far, overdoes the repetition, exceeds its expected limits, and actually results in the reverse of its intended goal.   But advertising strategies can be educational strategies.

The first of these strategies involves the creative or communication aspects of advertising.

## ADVERTISING CREATIVE STRATEGIES

Too often what advertising practitioners term the "creative" function is a misnomer because it is too narrow a focus.  Most of what advertising involves can be and should be creative: There can be creative messages and communications, but advertising can also involve creativity in many other functions—in originality of media planning and selection, innovations in management and direction, and imaginative research methods and applications.  Yet, for all its faults, there are lessons to be learned from advertising, as an examination of both its theoretical and applied aspects will show.

### Theoretical

Primary in any advertising communication theory is the necessity of knowing one's audience.  The direction, strategies and tactics of the campaign cannot be established unless and until the audience is well defined, well known, and well understood.  If any other approach is used that does not include this audience familiarity, the advertising campaign is doomed to failure, just as any instructional goal will fail unless the instruction is tailored to the recipient.

Many educators attempt to force knowledge, in the form of courses and curricula, into students' minds.  Some educators even go so far as to attempt to increase enrollments in their courses by requiring many or, ideally, from their point of view, all students to enroll in these courses as a requirement to earning a degree. Yet progressive and knowledgeable educators realize that the best way to increase enrollments is to make the courses attractive and interesting; the best way to encourage students to gain the knowledge from those courses is to provide something worthwhile that will enhance the students' lives and livelihood.  This approach, known as promising a benefit, is one of the hallmarks of successful message theory.

Advertisers know that people choose messages.  Audiences are bombarded with information and entertainment.  Advertisements contribute to this information overload: Estimates are that on the average day the average American is exposed to as many as 1500 or more advertisements.  From this surfeit of facts, trivia, propaganda and gossip, consumers must select, and their selection process is complicated.  First they select what they will be exposed to by their choices of publications and programs, then they select how they will perceive these messages, next they selectively retain some of the data from the volumes forced upon them, and finally they select services, products, and ideas for their own use. People select messages: They choose what advertising to see and hear just as they choose what lessons they will learn.

In advertising as in education, there is no Rosetta Stone.  Every discipline, every organization, every institution has its own jargon and acronyms. But to communicate, in education as in advertising, both sender and receiver must be using the same language at the same level.   Advertising is accused of communicating at a sixth-grade level, which is probably true.   But the reason behind that level of sophistication (or lack of sophistication, depending upon one's prejudices) is to provide useful information that can be easily understood without the resulting rejection.   Although this situation may not be entirely analogous to education, there are similarities: The teacher must use terminology and phraseology that his or her students comprehend and assimilate, else the learning process is short-circuited.   If the information of education is to be learned, remembered, and used, it must first be communicated, and again, the advertising communication strategy applies: Communicate with a common language at a common level of comprehension.

Comprehension also depends on agreement.   It is not necessary that the new knowledge, being acquired, harmonize exactly and precisely with everything that one already knows.   But it is requisite that this new information be able to fit within the existing knowledge structures. This is a basic premise of persuasion, one advocated even by Aristotle in the 4th century B.C. The information provided, whether by educator or by advertiser, cannot conflict too directly with the recipient's preconceptions. Concepts that are too far from a student's current knowledge base or too much in contrast with what he or she already believes, no matter how compelling or engaging, will simply not be adopted.

Personality also comes into play.   New material is assimilated most easily and most willingly when it relates to a personality need in some way or fashion.   A myriad of ideas and impressions surround each of us every day: Those that are adopted are those that relate to our own personalities and our own needs. Educators could learn this lesson from advertisers.

Effective advertisements close with a charge to act.   Attracting the audience, informing its members, interesting them in one's benefits, eliciting their desire, and convincing them they need what one is selling—all these can be lost unless it is explained to the recipients what they are expected to do.   If one of the last steps in creating an advertisement is a call for action, one of the final phases in inducing learning is to provide an application.   There is yet another consideration for successful theoretical communication strategies: group approval.   Students select majors and enroll in courses that garner group approval.   Audiences buy products and use services that gain this same group approval.   The secondary group must approve of what one already has and does. The primary group must approve of what one wants to become and accomplish.   For education and for advertising, approval by the primary and secondary groups of which the audience or class members are a part is vital.

Though these concepts may not first appear to be highly theoretical, they relate directly to theories of communication and persuasion as used in advertising message strategies.   Educators need to remind themselves of these basic theories.

## Applied

Repetition is an applied technique, and much of teaching and learning depends on repetition, just as does much of advertising.  The strength of repetition is awesome: When one's child sings his or her first song, solo, and it turns out to be a commercial jingle for beer, it demonstrates only too clearly, even fearsomely, the power of repetition.  But if repetition can teach a child to sing about a beer, it can also teach a child the alphabet.  If advertising commercial techniques provide easy access to a child's memory, those techniques can be transferred to educational purposes and uses.

So it is that "Sesame Street" has been such a success in educational TV.  Each program is "sponsored" by two letters of the alphabet and by one numeral.  Those letters and that number are repeated throughout the program, illustrated with poems, cartoons, jingles, jokes, and stories.  By the time the program hour is completed, so is the link to the children's memory.  If advertising can teach beer commercial jingles, it can also teach the alphabet—which it does every afternoon on PBS.

The motion of a TV commercial also educates.  Movement attracts.  It involves.  It links two or more things together, on the screen and in one's mind.  Motion can attract attention and direct that attention to what is important.  The success of MTV, with its juxtaposed, rapid-fire graphics, is eloquent testimony of what motion can do.

As an advertising medium, what is unique about TV is that it offers stimulation to two senses, sight and sound.  That combination, in sum, offers the unique quality and capability of demonstration.  It is boring to talk about something that one cannot see; it is difficult to imagine something that one cannot envision.  Demonstration overcomes these disadvantages.

And demonstration aids the educational process by adding involvement.  Having the television viewer singing along with the commercial is great, from the advertiser's perspective.  Providing motion to direct the audience's or class's attention is also helpful. Demonstrating relationships and interactions is powerfully instructive: Showing how a child's savings account brings financial awareness and responsibility along with the potential growth of funds is doubly informative and persuasive.  All these processes introduce the concept of involvement.  Spiriting away one's mind to cross new frontiers, see over new horizons—that is the essence of education.  A small child, playing on the floor in front of the TV set, suddenly stops and watches when the commercials come onto the screen. That may be disconcerting to parents, but it is the essence of involvement.  It is the kind of power that advertising exerts and that can and should be transferred to the process of education.

Music also carries power, as MTV amply demonstrates.  Humans incorporate an innate need for and appreciation of rhythm. Its regular presence calms and stimulates simultaneously, and the best TV commercials use rhythm by "cutting to the beat," changing the scenes in time with the background music.  Music is a common factor in advertising: setting the mood and tone, attracting the ear, reinforcing the theme. Indeed, everywhere students go— supermarkets, drugstores, sports events, even elevators, music is playing.  Except in the classroom.

## ADVERTISING MEDIA STRATEGIES

Not only message strategies, but also media strategies can be transferred from advertising to education. The most common elements of advertising media considerations are reach, frequency, impact, and continuity.  All four of these factors can be applied to educational processes as well.  Reach is the size of the audience or the percentage of some group with which one can communicate.  To "reach" an audience is to communicate and have effect; to "reach" a student is to break through the barriers effectively and communicate.  The similarity is obvious, as is the importance, for both education and for advertising.

The number of times that an advertising message is sent is termed frequency more specifically, frequency of insertion.   But more important, for both the advertiser and the educator, is the frequency of exposure, the number of times that the audience member receives that message.

The size of a printed advertisement and the length of a broadcast commercial are media measures of impact. But impact can also be gained through the use of message factors such as color, loudness, contrast, and shape, as well as through the use of size and length.   Burying important information in the middle of a long lecture dooms that information to obscurity.  Textbooks highlight important information, just as advertisements do.  But educators do not follow the lead of advertising by lengthening or shortening the message, by emphasizing through highlighting, by strengthening through simplifying.

The most overlooked factor, in advertising media strategies and perhaps also in educational strategies, is continuity.  The amazing fact about continuity is that it is free and easy: It does not necessarily cost the advertiser anything extra, and it does not necessarily require the educator to do anything extra.  It is only a matter of doing what is already planned, but simply changing the timing and consistency.

Continuity is the pattern of message presentation, the scheduling of the impressions, the lessons, the exposures, the courses. Frequency is communicating often, whether the same message or a different message. Repetition is communicating the same message, whether often or not. Continuity is the pattern, repeating, but not so frequently as to irritate or repulse; altering the frequency so as to reinforce by building upon previous lessons and knowledge, yet without excess.

## ADVERTISING RESPONSE

The traditional result of advertising has been purchase, but modern advertising desires more: a continuing relationship with the audience.   The sale is no longer the end result of an advertising campaign; instead, it is the beginning of a mutually beneficial relationship, wherein both the seller-advertiser and the buyer-audience benefit, at least potentially.   When either perceives that those benefits are no longer possible or desirable, the relationship is ended.

This modern marriage should also be the outcome of education.   Education is not simply kindergarten through high school, or a baccalaureate degree: Education is a lifelong process.   When one stops learning, one is dead, practically, if not actually.

In its traditional selling efforts, advertising has traditionally utilized a stimulus-response theory:  To sell food, show the finished meal, stimulate hunger, and bring on the hoped-for result, purchase.   In education, enough repetitions bring about the desired response, making small Pavlovian applications of many classroom situations: Rote and repetition can result in recall, repetition and, perhaps, even learning.

## CONCLUSIONS

Clearly advertising is a powerful educator.   Combining the powers of advertising and the mass media with the powers of education could produce a synergy that is larger and stronger than either or both of them.

Advertising is a relative newcomer, in many respects an outgrowth of other disciplines such as marketing, sociology, psychology and communication, but education has much to gain from advertising techniques.   Advertising is used because it works.   Outcomes are an essential part of advertising: Sponsors pay for it only because the results are worth it.   These same kinds of results and outcomes are potentially in store for education. Advertising can be a powerful educator.   And education can be a powerful user of advertising.

# 10

# The Betrayal of the Media

## Chester St. H. Mills and Rebecca A. Chaisson

### THE TRAGIC SENSE OF THE STEREOTYPE

Television commercials are designed around racial lines and represent a cultural bias. Anyone who watches American TV and sits through the commercials for any length of time will begin to see that a subtle, but consistent, racial stereotype emerges. The argument can thus be presented that the advertising media—with specific reference to the TV commercial—use ethnic groups for a specific purpose. The manner in which these groups are used subtly places them in roles and conditions that perpetuate a stereotype. Since the purpose of an advertising commercial is to sell a product, how it sells that product and the racial images it brings to the American screen can be perceived as an offensive and subliminal attempt to assign a group of people to a consistent underclass; or to influence individuals to consider their racial counterparts as inferior or superior; or to motivate groups of people to regard and see themselves as being persistently at the bottom of the American societal strata. Many people still remember an infamous edition of a long-distance telephone company's internal newsletter, circulated among employees a few years ago. Pictured with an article about long-distance calls to Africa was a dancing gorilla. The subliminal message was vicious and silent. The newsletter was quickly withdrawn, but not before the "other" message had been transmitted and the damage done.

In 1968, John Belinda, a Kiowa Navajo and Executive Director of the National Congress of American Indians, went before the New York City Commission on Human Rights to tell its members that "the enhancement and perpetuation of stereotype motifs of the Indian as drunken, savage, or treacherous, unreliable or childlike, produce impeding effects on employability of the Indian or his opportunities for education to a state of employability." "It also lends itself," he continued, "to the self-righteous justification on the part of the non-Indian in application of commercial activities which have direct social and economic impact on the Indian" (qtd. in Dallos, "American Indian Group" 94). As he continued to speak before the commission, Belinda cited a TV commercial for a children's breakfast food in which an Indian appeared in war paint, wearing a Buffalo hat with hems, jumping up and down and screaming. "This is the only picture the non-Indian gets of the Indian," he said. Again, the subliminal message in that TV commercial was vicious and silent.

What, too, is the psychological message adduced by the American viewer of Hispanic ancestry who watches a coffee commercial? He sees Juan Valdez—who is called *exigente* (an expert) in his country—appearing as a *campesino* (a peasant) on TV in a modern American supermarket with his serape on his shoulders, a machete in his hand, and his donkey beside him. Such a commercial may have been considered "cute" or perhaps even appropriate at the turn of the century, as was the handkerchief of Aunt Jemima or the picture of the "Gold Dust Twins" on boxes of cleanser. These ads may have sold the products, but they also stigmatized and relegated a group of people to a permanent niche in the societal structure. The subtleties of patterns portraying Latin Americans in ways such as these suggest that minorities seen or acting in TV commercials are placed in roles that do not remove them from such a banal image, since they are not yet considered part of the prevalent attitudes and values of the dominant society or group in this country.

Such an argument was disputed more than twenty-seven years ago by CBS Vice President for Programming Michael Dann. When Dann appeared before the New York City Commission for Human Rights in 1968, he explained that "the critical factor is that man who sits in that dark room with a typewriter." He continued his verbal disquisition before the commission by stating that "TV is escapism and likes to deal with America as it is for the most part. And for the most part there are not that many Negro judges, Negro governors, Negro senators. The producer or writer approaches the conceptual fact so as to reflect the scene as it is . . . . As a result, there had been some hesitation on the part of writers who sought to avoid 'artificial situations' " (qtd. in Dallos, "TV Explains" 62). These statements were made over against the damning statistical results published that same year by Richard Lemon in the *Saturday Evening Post*, a magazine that Dann should have read: "[O]nly 2.3 percent of all commercials used any blacks, Orientals, Puerto Ricans, or Indians" (qtd. in Dominick & Greenberg 22).

The fatuous logic of Dann's vapid remarks is apparent. "The Beverly Hillbillies," "I Dream of Jeannie," and "Bewitched" were TV programs of the sixties. So, too, were "Have Gun, Will Travel" and "Gunsmoke." One doubts that any of these programs then, or any of the Saturday morning TV shows for children now, dealt with life in America as it actually was. When Dann was then told by the commission's counsel that "there are many Negro physicians and district attorneys . . . even Negro mayors of two major cities" and that "the Negro could easily be depicted in everyday life," he replied that "when there are two mayors of roughly a thousand large cities, even if you were playing Russian roulette, the odds are that the mayor of a city on TV won't be a Negro (qtd. in Dallos, "TV Explains" 62).

Dann failed to realize that more than 10 percent of the American population, including some whose ancestors had fought in the American Revolution and in the American Civil War, were listening to or reading his words, which were excluding them from the mainstream of American life. The total struggle and accomplishments—against all odds—of a noble people were now to be written out of history and thought of as superfluous, as an "artificial situation." There can be little doubt that TV commercials have created, and to this day still create, an unconscious structure by which viewers of visible color evaluate their particular racial position in today's multicultural society. Eight years later, in 1976, Charlotte O'Kelly and Linda Bloomquist published their findings on women and African Americans on TV. They constructed a content analysis of programs and commercials according to type of appeal. Their results revealed that the shows and the commercials tended to be the most biased in favor of males and whites.

Since 1977, Ronald F. Bush, Paul J. Solomon and Joseph F. Hair, Jr. have measured the representation of African Americans on TV commercials and have argued that their presence is high and is in proportion to the population in the country.   George Zinkham, William Quails, and Abhiji Biswas, looking at advertisements in magazines and on TV from 1946 to 1986, have supported the findings of Bush, Solomon, and Hair. They, too, argue that "black representation in all advertisements (both magazine and TV) has increased significantly over time. In addition, there appear to be significant media differences, with more black actors appearing on television than in magazine ads" (552). But these researchers deal only with content analyses and, thus, with quantifiable results; not with the psychological effect the commercial has on these minority viewers, or with the societal impact the TV image has on the family life of the viewer, on identity, or on the American value system. Michael Jordan, for example, runs not through the streets of Beverly Hills, but through the desert, the hills, and the valleys of what seems to be a third-world country. We see him almost stepping on somebody's valuable chicken in his hurry to discover the meaning of life; to find out that life is nothing more than a sport to be drunk up. If John Condry is right, that "watching the ads apparently influences what children think and feel about certain specific products" (211), why not have a known Hispanic brain surgeon or a Native American philosopher discuss the meaning of life? So Michael will run and continue to run; and as he runs over hill, over dale, and across the dusty trail, the remarks of Ossie Davis at a conference at the University of Michigan, that such images are used as an instrument of social control, reverberate in the mind of the perceiver (Jackson 61). "The way in which individuals are portrayed," further argue Anthony Jackson and Deborah Cherniss, "determines to an important extent the way they are treated" (14).

Take another example: the Saturn Commercial that General Motors uses on TV to sell its product. It would seem from that commercial that minorities who buy a Saturn automobile can go to the company picnic. If Russ, the service manager, is there, he will lead you and a group of picnickers to the well-lit underbelly of the Saturn and explain all the intricacies of the automobile.  It would also seem from another commercial provided by the company that the highest level the minority worker can reach in that company is to be able to pull the chain to stop the production line. If this commercial represents the degree of accomplishment and the level of achievement the person of visible color can attain, then the American dream for minorities is as gloomy as the Dickensian interior of that factory and will never be realized.

Now that we are coming to the end of the 20th century, we still seem to be stuck in the quagmire of racism, racial stereotyping, and psychological brainwashing because American advertisers and advertising agencies have failed to use one of the most persuasive methods for bringing a nation of diverse people together. Instead, TV commercials are used to divide, to create, and to maintain in this country an environment that is separate, hostile, and unequal. To this day African Americans are still represented on TV as caricatures of Amos and Andy—happy-go-lucky and unreliable (Dominick and Greenberg)—Hispanics as "illegals," Native Americans as drunks, and Asian Americans as math whizzes or experts in martial arts. It has become difficult to dispel these views, which remain today to be continued and repeated in the 21st century. It should be the responsibility of advertisers and those of the Madison Avenue ilk to become sensitive to the intrinsic feelings of racial groups who might now be offended by commercials on TV that neither represent them nor portray them as part of the mainstream of American life. Thus, commercials still pack the punch of racial prejudice, despite any statement to the contrary, for little or nothing has been done to change the depiction of minorities in these ads. On the surface, this representation of reality is designed to seem inclusive, but such is not the case. Under the surface is the harsh reality that through these ads the people of visible color are manipulated so they remain hermetically sealed and disconnected from the mainstream of American life. What has changed, however, is the sophistication of the manipulation; and this sophisticated exclusion of minorities also extends to the stereotyping and exclusion of all women in America, whose sole role in the commercial, it seems, is to sell diapers, deodorant, household products, or feminine napkins.

We must therefore keep in mind the purpose of an ad. It is the language of capitalism, whose message is to make money. Everyone heeds the message or is drawn to it in some way. No one is immune from its siren call. However, as scholars, when we take up our pens, we sometimes ignore the fundamental issue associated with the problem of inclusion, which is also inherent in the message. We see through the glass darkly as we embrace our scholarship and assume our intellectual stance. Then we gape at the issue, begin our dialectic, and explain away the message through the roseate glasses of some arcane theories. We become scholarly, objective, and detached. In doing so, do we discount the struggle of the African American, the Asian, the Hispanic, and the Native American for inclusion? O'Kelly and Bloomquist note in their article, "Women and Blacks on TV," that "media's main influence is reinforcement rather than change or conversion. People seek out, pay attention to, and remember that which is consistent with their already existing ways of thinking and, conversely, tend to ignore, avoid, or forget that which disagrees with the ideas they already hold. Furthermore, the greater salience the idea, belief, or behavior has for the person, the more these generalizations tend to hold" (183).

Although Madison Avenue has "come a long way" since 1968 by including more minorities in commercials (Bush, Solomon, & Hair 1977), it is doubtful if the numbers of minorities in the commercials we see represent a more "mainstream" approach. Michael Jackson and Ray Charles have appeared in Pepsi commercials, and several McDonald's commercials have used African Americans and Asians in their TV ads. AT&T uses a young, charming, and attractive actress (perhaps of Hispanic ancestry) as well as other people of visible color in its commercials to promulgate its "no circles" program. Certainly the paradigm has changed if we are simply to look at numbers—although the appearance of Hispanics in TV commercials is virtually nil (Wilkes & Valencia). There may be more blacks in TV commercials, according to Bush, Solomon, and Hair, but this phenomenon is due to the pressure put on advertising agencies in the Sixties by civil rights groups and by the Federal Communications Commission (FCC) to end discrimination in advertising. The end results have remained the same. Nothing has changed, really. The number of minorities in commercials may have increased on TV, but few minorities play an important role in the commercial theme or layout. Only recently has Charles Barkley been shown in the foreground of a Right Guard commercial, actually holding the product and speaking about it. How absurd he looks in his tweeds in the role of an Egyptologist with an English accent is another matter. Most minorities are given minor roles of average or little importance to the theme of the commercial or background roles where they appear for a little bit longer than a nanosecond or blend in with the crowd and are hard to find. The distressing conditions that J. David Colfax and Susan Sternberg discuss in their study of the perpetuation of racial stereotypes in mass circulation magazine advertisements are just as valid today for the TV commercial. Remember that Ray Charles and Michael Jackson are in the music business. Colfax and Sternberg state:

We would suggest that . . . the representation of blacks in this manner cannot be taken as a sign of an "improvement" in the depicted status of the black American. In the first place, the stereotype of the "Negro musician" is a pervasive and frequently derogatory cultural stereotype, and it would be fatuous to suggest that the "black musician" occupies, in terms of dominant cultural values, a position equivalent to that of blacks in other "white collar" occupations such as, say, accountancy or schoolteaching. The professional "pop" musician—black or white—occupies a marginal, if not deviant status in the American social and occupational hierarchy. Thus advertisers who depict blacks in these roles symbolically encapsulate them, both occupationally and socially, cutting them off from conventional occupational mobility routes—routes which represent, to many whites, the most threatening aspect of race in American society. Since, as the myth has it, musical talent cannot be "achieved," the fact that musical talent is the predominant characteristic of depicted blacks only serves to reinforce the cultural stereotype and neutralizes whatever threat might have been implicit in the depiction of blacks in more conventional white collar roles. (11)

Even with all the things written about the media, it is still apparent that they have not learned from their mistakes. They have not yet learned how to include all people in an expanding American mosaic. The "moral imperative" that organizational expert Taylor Cox, Jr., of the University of Michigan discusses in his work has become, instead, a moral dilemma. In their attempt to rectify a thorny issue, the advertising pundits continue their deception by creating new commercials, which they think will appeal separately to each racial group. Some beer commercials as well as soft drink commercials seem to be moving in this direction, and the sponsors seem oblivious to the effect these "separate but equal" commercials will have on the minority viewer. The product will be sold, but unless the ad for that product includes all Americans, it will continue the stereotype and keep unrepresented groups in their racial and cultural place. Thus, the moral imperative—"do it because it is right"—becomes supplanted by financial exigency—"do it because it is profitable."

## DECEPTIVE IMAGES OF WOMEN, CHILDREN, AND MINORITIES IN TV ADVERTISING

According to Condry, the business of the TV industry is to sell to audiences who have little in common except that they are "tuned in" at the same time. The television industry then "sells" the audience to advertisers interested in selling values and products. These advertisers support and sustain gender stereotypes, which affect individual ideas about self, about identity and power valuations in men and women, in children, and in minorities. As the advertisers sustain these stereotypes, they make an impact on the sociocultural values and messages that engender an array of mental health problems. Women, for example, identify with models on the Jenny Craig, Slim Fast, Sweet Success, and Thigh Master commercials as they seek to obtain what they see in the advertisement as their ideal weight and shape. At the same time, women are cast in commercials that advertise Shake and Bake, Potatoes Express, Rice-a-Roni, Campbell Soups, and other foods that have either a high  sodium or a high fat content. Women also identify with commercials that tell them to make sure that they provide a variety of foods for their families.

These mixed-message commercials are a setup for depression and anxiety as women slim fast for breakfast, enjoy sweet success at lunch, and shake and bake for dinner. The stereotype created by television dieters communicates to women that they can have improved self-image and self-esteem if they use the advertised products. This stereotype is a myth and many women report sadness and frustration about regaining the weight they lost on  one of the quick-fix diets advertised on TV. As Attic and Brooks-Gunn argue, "Dieting typically does not result in lower weight, but in fatigue, irritability, [and] chronic hunger" (219).

Philip Myers and Frank Biocca have also studied TV advertising and its effects on body-image distortions in young women. They found that watching even thirty minutes of TV advertising altered a woman's perception of the shape of her body.

Body-size distortion is a common phenomenon associated with eating disorders. Myers and Biocca also found a shift in both mood and attitude in the women studied in their sample. Mood and attitude swings are common with eating-disordered patients. Perhaps advertisers do not think of the consequences of the superficial messages portrayed as they advertise their "miracle" products. It is nearly impossible to maintain the slender figures shown in TV commercials with the other conflicting messages given to women who must be caretakers and helpers, nurturers, all giving and all knowing when it comes to matters in the home. Mixed-message commercials can cause mental distress and provoke symptoms related to eating disorders. Such disorders are associated with self-nurturing and emotional management.

Another issue related to women's identity and TV advertising is the popularity of color contact lenses, which were advertised to make "brown eyes blue." The introduction of that product communicated to women that eye color was important and that they had to keep changing their external appearance in order to look attracive. Women bought this ad hook, line, and sinker and dug deep into their pocketbooks to look different. Some of the color lenses unfortunately made some women look like zombies, and many groups in the African-American community saw the selling of eye color as a selling out of brown-eyed African-American pride and identity. From a psychosocial development standpoint, one wonders what kind of developmental crisis was created by this type of advertising. Was there an identity crisis here? Were women not good enough, attractive enough? Did the color of one's eyes become so boring to someone else? Why weren't men seen in these ads?

The ad on color contact lenses does not seem to appear as often as it used to, but one wonders about the type of advertising malfeasance that someone will try on women next. Somehow these advertisers must feel that their commercials must be designed to move women back to earlier stages in their development. They must return to the little-girl-straight-body shapes. Women, no fat please; and change your eye color frequently! How's that for preconception regression?

A commercial on a hair depilatory product for women was shown only on New Orleans TV. In this commercial, the advertising preacher suggested that we remove the hair from our legs, since they look too disgusting with hair on them. The preacher further suggested that men will not like hairy-legged women and that the woman will find herself and her legs unattractive. The preacher went on to imply that other women will talk about the viewer's legs, too. Here, again, is another way that TV advertising tampers with the self-concept and identity of women. Real women have shaved legs and shaved underarms. Does the reader ever remember seeing a man advertising leg-shaving products? Maybe the South is so traditional that advertising here is used to keep women and men in more stereotypical and traditional roles.

Numerous studies examine gender stereotyping in commercials in the United States. Some of the studies in other countries report the same thing: that women are portrayed in subservient roles and men are portrayed as authority figures or experts.

Over the years, advertisers have probably thought that they were providing equal rights to women by increasing the number of women in commercials. Yes, there has been an increase. However, this increase is offset by the roles that women portray. Women continue to represent food, feminine products, and household cleaning items. They speak to animals, children, and babies. The message transmitted to TV viewers is that women are important for cleaning and caring for the sick, for young children, and for men. While all of this work is going on, women must also look good—which means thin—and they must not smell. Advertisers are keen at remediating these problems by selling numerous weight-loss products such as Sweet Success, cleaning products such as Mr. Clean, quick-fix appliances like Mr. Coffee, and "smell fragrant" products like Summer's Eve and FDS. Some women would rather Mr. Clean be present in person and Mr. Coffee in the flesh. This kind of help in the house and kitchen would be much more desirable and effective. Advertisers also sell Obsession, Coco, and Opium, fragrances designed to keep women smelling good enough to hook and keep that man. But there is the implied message that if a woman fails to use these products, she might offend someone with body fat, dirty floors, rumpled skin, and a smelly body.

It is almost impossible to protect children from the ravages of TV advertising. TV marketing for children is irresponsible. Children are being seduced into eating Count Chocula, Kaboom, Trix, Fruit Pebbles, and numerous other cereals that are high in sugar and low in nutritional value. It is no wonder that children eat doughnuts and sweet rolls for breakfast these days. They are accustomed to sugary breakfast foods. Obesity, which usually results from poor diet choices and inactivity, continues to be a problem for elementary school children (Heit & Meeks).

Even the National Education Goals for the year 2000 spell out the importance of children receiving the nutrition and physical activity experiences that make them ready to learn. Can Cap'n Crunch and Jello Jiggles prepare the American child for the educational environment? Generally, sugary and high-fat foods are basically junk. They do not provide the kind of nutritional fortitude that enables children to stay focused on learning. The school lunch and school breakfast programs for children are important for them. The advertising media can certainly assist these children by teaching them to make healthy food choices.

As mentioned earlier, physical activity experiences for children are listed in the National Education Goals. They are also included in Healthy People 2000, the national initiative developed by the Institute of Medicine of the National Academy of Sciences and by the United States Public Health Service. Sometimes the only physical activity that children experience is the movement produced by pressing the remote control button of the TV, Nintendo, or Gameboy. Many parents report that children would rather watch TV or play with Nintendo and Gameboy than venture outside to play ball or just play freely with other children. Schools report that only 36 percent of students in grades one through twelve are enrolled in physical education throughout high school (Heit & Meeks). Yet we keep hearing that as adults we need to exercise at least three times weekly for twenty minutes. As adults, we struggle with this type of physical activity schedule while children establish a behavior pattern at a young age that will have an impact on them for the rest of their lives. Some of these patterns are related to poor nutrition and to physical inactivity and are preventable in today's youth. One wonders what we are doing to our children when they pressure parents to buy them what they see on TV in a nicely packaged commercial. Are advertisers so invested in making the dollar that they do so at any price?

Gender stereotyping is also common in TV advertising aimed at children. Although little has been published about sex-role portrayals in commercials aimed at children, one can simply ask about the last time a male child was seen on TV playing with dolls and non-electronic games. When was a female child seen advertising toy cars and toy planes? Barrie Gunter reports that there was a preponderance of male characters in commercials aimed at children. She suggests that even imaginary roles of boys and girls were highly stereotyped.

In 1978, Nick Johnson, a former commissioner of the FCC, stated, "All of television is educational . . . the only question is what does it teach?" (qtd. in Condry 102). Twenty years later we still keep wondering why Johnnie can't read, why our children are killing each other, and why we have sexually active young boys and girls. Yes, some of this is learned in the home. There is no denying that parents are their children's first teachers. Nevertheless, plenty of the information learned by children is learned from TV, with advertising as one of the key institutions in the transmission of values to the larger society. Although the church, the school, and the family are the transmitters of values, none of these institutions has the power that TV advertising has in terms of scope and repetitiveness (Pollay). Advertising has great universal influence, and our children are being educated by TV, with many of their values being shaped by the creators of these commercials.

Even the TV station that was designed for children has been a disappointment. One study (Wulfemeyer & Mueller) analyzed Whittle's Channel One commercials. The results showed that the personal values stressed most often in Channel One commercials were leisure/pleasure, appearance, sexuality, wisdom, and independence. The authors of this study discovered that the dominant themes found in the commercials were having friends, having fun, and being attractive. The majority of the commercials stressed the product value of effectiveness of technological superiority and downplayed such values as uniqueness and inexpensiveness. One disturbing finding in this study was the lack of African-American, Hispanic-American, Native American, and Asian-American models in Channel One commercials. This was especially disturbing since 80 percent of the schools participating in the study were racially mixed. When we think about identity development and self-concept, it is difficult to conceptualize how children who watch Channel One will become decent and caring human beings who assess others by content of character. The values transmitted—even by this school channel—are undesirable. We keep asking why children want to play so much and why they are concerned about their appearance and their sexual expression. We certainly get an answer from the messages expressed through advertising.

One area that has been given plenty of attention in TV advertising in the last five years or so is anti-drug commercials. One of these commercials was designed for the African-American community. It compared drug addiction to slavery. Recently the Red Dog beer commercial appeared on TV, with the dog as central character. This commercial is a reminder of the Joe Camel cigarette advertising seen on billboards throughout the country and the Spuds Mackenzie dog. Generally animals get the attention of children. So, again, we have the mixed message about drug and alcohol use. One set of commercials tells children not to use drugs, that they are deadly. Another set of commercials shows animals along with alcohol and cigarettes. Still other commercials clearly show young people drinking alcoholic beverages. These commercials are a subliminal demonstration to children that adulthood includes drinking for fun. But when young children try to emulate adulthood, we tell them "Just Say No" or "Say When," or "It isn't Miller time yet."

One less talked about area of TV advertising and children is the increased conflict that results between parent and child (Condry). Effective commercials encourage children to believe that they should have what is advertised in order to have more fun and enjoy play. Parents rarely see this type of coercion in the same way and are at a loss, especially with young children who cannot cognitively understand the gimmickry of advertising. Some parents argue with children, while others purchase advertised toys in order to keep children from experiencing distress from not having what they want. There is nothing sadder than parents who compensate for poverty and lack of quality time with children by providing them with expensive toys that have been advertised on TV.

The absence of minorities in commercials aimed at youth on Channel One is not unique. Although African Americans have increased in some advertisements, the portrayal of African Americans continues to be stereotyped. Hispanic Americans, Native Americans, and Asian Americans are definitely under-represented compared to the national population. The images that ethnic minorities portray definitely assign them to certain products and services and thus to certain roles.

The lack of minorities in some commercials makes them virtually invisible and their needs unimportant. Let's take hair-care product commercials seen on the major networks as an example. Vidal Sassoon, Pantene, and L'Oreal commercials use Caucasian women to show their products. What does this mean? "If you don't look good, we don't look good," says a male voice-over in the Vidal Sassoon commercial. "I use Preference by L'Oreal and I am worth it," says the blonde model on that commercial. Does the commercial suggest that the hair of African-American, Hispanic-American, Native American, and Asian-American models does not look good enough to make Sassoon look good? Or maybe there are not any black, Hispanic, or Asian women out there who are worthy of L'Oreal hair-care products? These products communicate to women that hair that is long, flowing, bouncy, and preferably blonde is more desirable than short, curly, kinky, dark hair. Braids, corn rows, and short, curly, or kinky hair have never been advertised on the major networks for viewers. Perhaps the hair of minority groups does not represent the image that advertisers want to sell.

Generally, minority women can analyze these commercials and use other value representations to choose products that are better for them. But what about children from these groups? How do these commercials with white models make minority children feel about their racial identity? Clearly if one group is made to look superior to or better than another group, the second group would most likely emulate the first group. All one has to do is look at the children on programs such as "Star Search" to see young children with hairstyles that mirror the styles of the adult women seen in these ads. Children have hair that is relaxed, spritzed, and permed so that they can have visual starlike quality. When will braids, corn rows, and short, curly, wavy, kinky, and bone-straight hair make a debut in advertising? These comments are not intended to ask for more of these products for women. As was mentioned earlier, women are sold too many products that reinforce stereotypes, and hair-care products represent some of the reinforcement. When minority women watch TV, they see that racial identity is connected to certain ornaments, a specific look, and a specific behavior that exclude them. This exclusion has a greater impact on their children because children become vulnerable when they are excluded and are made to feel as if they do not fit the TV image.

When it comes to advertising hair-care products on TV, some men are also excluded. For years, African-American men, and other men who had thick, curly facial hair, could not use the same shaving products and equipment. Advertisers showed their products as though they were universally beneficial. Only recently has one company showed a razor that also works for men with coarse curly hair and included all racial types of American men in its commercials.

TV advertising in no way honors and validates the uniqueness of minorities in this country. It fails them by its sins of omission and commission. It fails women and men by creating and sustaining unhealthy and unreasonable stereotypes. What a sad commentary! Such a powerful institution like advertising could contribute much harmony in this country. Unfortunately, TV advertising has its own way of alienating Americans.

## WORKS CITED

Attic, I., and J. Brooks-Gunn. "Weight Concerns as Chronic Stressors in Woman." *Gender and Stress.* Ed. R. Bamett, Lois Biener, and Grace Baruch. New York: Free Press, 1987. 218-254.

Bush, Ronald F., Paul J. Solomon, and Joseph F. Hair, Jr. "There Are More Blacks in TV Commercials." *Journal of Advertising* 17 (1977): 21–25.

Colfax, J. David, and Susan Sternberg. "The Perpetuation of Racial Stereotypes: Blacks in Mass Circulation Magazine Advertisements." *Public Opinion Quarterly* 36, 1 (Spring 1972): 8-18.

Condry, John C. *The Psychology of Television.* Hillsdale, N.J.: Lawrence Erlbaum Associates Inc., 1989.

Dallos, Robert E. "TV Explains Lack of Negro Roles." *New York Times* 16 Mar. 1968: 62.

————. "American Indian Group Accuses Several Media of Discrimination." *New York Times* 22 Mar. 1968: 94.

Davis, Ossie. "Where Are the Black Image-Makers Hiding?" *Black Families and the Medium of Television.* Ed. Anthony W. Jackson. Ann Arbor: University of Michigan Press, 1982.

Dominick, Joseph R., and Bradley S. Greenberg. "Three Seasons of Blacks on Television." *Journal of Advertising Research* 10. 2 (April 1970): 21-27.

Gunter, Barrie. *Television and Sex Role Stereotyping,.* London: John Libbey & Company, Ltd., 1986.

Heit, Philip, and Linda Meeks. *The Comprehensive School Health Education Curriculum.* Blacklick, Ohio: Meeks Heit Publishing Co., 1995.

Jackson, Anthony W., ed. *Black Families and the Medium of Television.* Ann Arbor: University of Michigan Press, 1982.

Lee, Bun E., and Louis A. Browne. "Effects of Television Advertising on African American Teenagers." *Journal of Black Studies* 25. 5 (May 1995): 523-36.

Lemon, Richard. "Black is the Color of TV's Newest Stars." *Saturday Evening Post* 30 Nov. 1968: 42-44.

Myers, Philip N., and Frank Biocca. "The Elastic Body Image: The Effect of Television Advertising and Programming on Body Image Distortions in Young Women." *Journal of Communication* 42. 3 (1992): 108-33.

O'Kelly, Charlotte G., and Linda Bloomquist. "Women and Blacks on TV." *Journal of Communications* (Autumn 1976): 179-84.

Pollay, Richard. "Measuring the Cultural Values Market in Advertising." *Current Issues and Research in Advertising* 1 (1983): 77-92.

Wilkes, Robert E., and Humberto Valencia. "Hispanics and Blacks in Television Commercials." *Journal of Advertising* 18. 1 (1989): 19-25.

Wulfemeyer, K. Tim, and Barbara Mueller. "Channel One and Commercials in Classrooms: Advertising Content Aimed at Students." *Journalism Quarterly* 69.3 (Autumn 1992): 724-42.

Zinkhan, George M., William J. Quails, and Abhijit Biswas. "The Use of Blacks in Magazine and Television Advertising: 1946 to 1986." *Journalism Quarterly* 67.3 (Autumn 1990): 547-53.

# Selected Bibliography

Allport, G.W. *The Nature of Prejudice.* Reading, Mass.: Addison Wesley Publishing Company, 1954.

"America's Corporate Flag-Waving Rednecks Redux." *The Economist* 21–27 July 1990: 68+.

Arlen, Michael. *Thirty Seconds.* New York: Farrar, Strauss and Giroux, 1980.

Atwood, Margaret. "Happy Endings." *Sudden Fiction International.* Ed. Robert Shapard and James Thomas. New York: W. W. Norton, 1989.

"Avant-Garde Unites Over Burroughs." *The New York Times* 1 December 1978: C11.

Barthes, Roland. "Myth Today." *Mythologies.* Trans. Annette Lavers. New York: Hill and Wang, 1975: 109–59.

Baudrillard, Jean. "Simulacra and Simulations." *Selected Writings.* Ed. Mark Poster. Stanford: Stanford University Press, 1988: 166–84.

"Beat Godfather Meets Glitter Mainman: William Burroughs, Say Hello to David Bowie." *Rolling Stone* 155 (28 February 1974): 24–27.

Beattie, Ann. "Snow." *Sudden Fiction International.* Ed. Robert Shapard and James Thomas. New York: W. W. Norton, 1989.

Bergen, D.J. and J.E.Williams. "Sex Stereotypes in the United States Revisited: 1972-1988." *Sex Roles* 24 (1991):413–23.

Bernstein, Basil. "A Public Language: Some Sociological Implications of a Linguistic Form." *British Journal of Sociology* 10 (1959): 311–25.

Bersani, Leo. *The Culture of Redemption.* Cambridge: Harvard University Press, 1990.

Best, Steven and Douglas Kellner. *Postmodern Theory: Critical Interrogations.* New York: The Guilford Press, 1991.

Blonsky, Marshall. *American Mythologies.* New York: Oxford University Press, 1992.

Borgmann, Albert. *Crossing the Postmodern Divide*. Chicago: University of Chicago Press, 1992.

Bretl, D.J. and J. Cantor. "The Portrayal of Men and Women in U.S. Television Commercials." *Sex Roles* 18 (1988): 595–609.

Buell, Lawrence. "American Pastoral Ideology Reappraised." *American Literary History* 1 (Spring 1989): 1–29.

Burroughs, William S. "The Cut-Up Method of Brion Gysin." *Yugen* 8 (1962): 31–35.

_____. *Edinburgh Conference Proceedings*. 24 August 1962: 18.

_____. *Junkie*. New York: Ace, 1953.

_____. *Naked Lunch*. New York: Grove Press, 1959.

CAIR (Council on American-Islamic Relations) Press Release. "DoubleTree Hotel Chain Alters TV Ads Deemed Offensive to Muslims." 16 March 1995.

Caplan, P.J. and J.B.Caplan. *Thinking Critically About Research on Sex and Gender*. New York: Harper Collins, 1994.

Cohen, Ira J. "Introduction to the Transaction Edition." *General Economic History* by Max Weber. New Brunswick, N.J.: Transaction Books, 1981.

Cohen, Robert. "Dispatches from the Interzone." *The New York Times Book Review*. 15 January 1995: 9.

Collins, Jim. *Uncommon Cultures: Popular Culture and Post-Modernism*. New York: Routledge, 1989.

Debord, Guy. *Society of the Spectacle*. Detroit: Black & Red, 1983.

Derrida, Jacques. "Structure, Sign and Place in the Discourse of the Human Sciences." *The Structuralist Controversy*. Ed. Richard Macksey and Eugenio Donato. Baltimore: Johns Hopkins University Press, 1970.

Dyer, Gillian. *Advertising as Communication*. London: Methuen, 1982.

Elliott, Stuart. "Companies Go for the Gold, Using Ambush Marketing." *The New York Times* 3 Feb. 1992: D1+.

Empson, William. *Some Versions of Pastoral*. 1934; rpt. New York: New Directions, 1974.

Ewen, Stuart. *All Consuming Images: The Politics of Style in Contemporary Culture*. New York: Basic Books, 1988.

Foster, Hal, ed. *The Anti-Aesthetic: Essays on Postmodern Culture*. Port Townsend, Wash.: Bay Press, 1983.

Fox, Stephen. *The Mirror Makers: A History of American Advertising and Its Creators*. New York: William Morrow, 1984.

Fromm, Erich. *The Forgotten Language: An Introduction to the Understanding of Dreams, FairyTales, and Myths*. New York: Grove Press, 1957.

Frye, Northrop. *Anatomy of Criticism: Four Essays*. Princeton: Princeton University Press, 1957.

Gitlin, Todd. "Car Commercials and *Miami Vice*: We Build Excitement." *Watching Television*. Ed. Todd Gitlin. New York: Pantheon, 1987: 136–61.

_____. "Hip-Deep in Postmodernism." *The New York Times Book Review.* 6 November 1988: 1, 35–36.

_____. "Postmodernism: Roots and Politics." *Cultural Politics in Contemporary America* . Ed. Ian Angus and Sut Jhally. New York: Routledge, 1989: 347–60.

Goffman, Erving. *Gender Advertisements.* New York: Harper and Row, 1979.

Goldberger, Paul. "25 Years of Unabashed Elitism." *The New York Times* 2 Feb. 1992: II, 1, 34.

Goldman, Robert. *Reading Ads Socially.* London and New York: Routledge, 1992.

Green, Harvey. *Fit for America.* Baltimore: Johns Hopkins, 1988.

Harvey, David. *The Condition of Postmodernity: An Inquiry into the Origins of Cultural Change.* Oxford: Basil Blackwell, 1989.

Hebdige, Dick. *Hiding in the Light: On Images and Things.* London: Routledge, 1988.

_____. *Subculture: The Meaning of Style.* 1979. London: Routledge, 1988.

Hesse, Hermann. *The Glass Bead Game.* Trans. Richard and Clara Winston. New York: Holt,Rinehart and Winston, 1969.

Hirschman, Albert O. *The Passions and the Interests: Political Arguments for Capitalism Before Its Triumph.* Princeton: Princeton University Press, 1977.

Hume, David. "Of Refinement in the Arts." *Writings on Economics.* Ed. E. Rotwein. Madison, Wis.: University of Wisconsin Press, 1970.

Hunter, James Davison. *Culture Wars: The Struggle to Define America.* New York: Basic Books, 1991.

Hutcheon, Linda. *The Politics of Postmodernism: History, Theory, Fiction.* London: Routledge, 1989.

Jameson, Frederic. "Postmodernism and Consumer Society." *Amerika Studien* (1984): 55–73.

_____. "Postmodernism, or the Cultural Logic of Late Capitalism." *The New Left Review* 146 (July–August 1984): 53–92.

_____. *Postmodernism or the Cultural Logic of Late Capitalism.* Durham, N.C .: Duke University Press, 1991.

Jencks, Charles. *Post-Modernism: The New Classicism in Art and Architecture.* New York: Rizzoli, 1987.

Joyce, James. *A Portrait of the Artist as a Young Man. The Portable James Joyce.* New York: The Viking Press, 1966.

Jung, Carl G. et al. *Man and His Symbols.* Garden City, N.Y.: Doubleday, 1964.

Kanner, Beatrice. "Orbiting Saturn." *New York* 15 April 1991: 14–19.

Kaplan, E. Ann. "Introduction." *Postmodernism and Its Discontents: Theories, Practices.* London: Verso, 1988.

_____. *Rocking Around the Clock: Music Television, Postmodernism, & Consumer Culture.* 1987. New York: Routledge, 1988.

Kline, Morris. *Mathematics: The Loss of Certainty.* New York: Oxford University Press, 1980.

Kroker, Arthur, Marilouise Kroker, and David Cook. *Panic Encyclopedia: the definitive guide to the postmodern scene*. New York: St. Martin's Press, 1989.

Lasch, C. *The Culture of Narcissism*. New York: Warner Books, 1979.

Lears, T.J. Jackson. "From Salvation to Self-Realization: Advertising and the Therapeutic Roots of Consumer Culture, 1880–1930." *The Culture of Consumption: Critical Essays in American History 1880–1980*. Ed. Richard Wightman Fox and T.J. Jackson Lears. New York: Pantheon Books, 1983: 3–38.

———. *Fables of Abundance: A Cultural History of Advertising in America*. New York: Basic Books, 1994.

Lehman, D. *Signs of the Times: Deconstruction and The Fall of Paul de Man*. New York: Poseiden Press, 1991.

Lerner, Laurence. *The Uses of Nostalgia: Studies in Pastoral Poetry*. London: Chatto and Windus, 1972.

Lévi-Strauss, Claude. *The Raw and the Cooked: Introduction to a Science of Mythology I*. Trans. John and Doreen Weightman. New York and Evanston: Harper & Row, 1969.

Leymore, Varda Langholz. *Hidden Myth: Structure and Symbolism in Advertising*. New York: Basic Books, 1975.

Lingeman, Richard. "A Consonance of Towns," in *Making America: The Society and Culture of the United States*. Ed. Luther S. Luedtke. Chapel Hill: University of North Carolina Press, 1992: 95–109.

Lippert, Barbara. "That Vision Thing: President Bush Implores Foreigners to See a Cut-Rate USA." *Adweek* 13 Jan. 1992: 24.

Lyotard, Jean-François. "Answering the Question: What Is Postmodernism?" Trans. Regis Durand. *The Postmodern Condition: A Report on Knowledge*. Trans. Geoff Bennington and Brian Massumi. Minneapolis: University of Minnesota Press, 1984: 71–84.

———. *The Postmodern Condition: A Report on Knowledge*. Trans. Geoff Bennington and Brian Massumi. Minneapolis: University of Minnesota Press, 1984.

Machor, James L. *Pastoral Cities: Urban Ideals and the Symbolic Landscape of America*. Madison: University of Wisconsin Press, 1987.

Marchand, Roland. *Advertising the American Dream: Making Way for Modernity 1920–1940*. Berkeley and Los Angeles: University of California Press, 1985.

Martin, Stephen-Paul. "Gallery." *The Literary Review* 3.4 (Summer 1990): 450–51.

McHale, Brian. *Postmodernist Fiction*. New York: Methuen, 1987.

McLuhan, Marshall, and Quentin Fiore. *The Medium Is the Message*. New York: Bantam, 1967.

Meisel, Perry. *The Myth of the Modern: A Study in British Literature and Criticism after 1850*. London and New Haven: Yale University Press, 1987.

Meyrowitz, Joshua. *No Sense of Place: The Impact of Electronic Media on Social Behavior*. New York: Oxford University Press, 1985.

Miller, Mark Crispin. *Boxed In: The Culture of TV*. Evanston, Ill.: Northwestern University Press, 1988.

____. "Political Ads: Decoding Hidden Messages." *Columbia Journalism Review*. Jan.-Feb. 1992: 36–39.

____. "Prime Time: Deride and Conquer." *Watching Television*. Ed. Todd Gitlin. New York: Pantheon, 1987: 193–228.

Mitchell, W.J.T. "Interview with Barbara Kruger." *Critical Inquiry* 17 (Winter 1991): 434–48.

Mueller, Claus. "Class as the Determinant of Political Communication." *American Media and Mass Culture: Left Perspectives*. Ed. Donald Lazere. Berkeley: University of California Press, 1988: 431–40.

Nash, Christopher. *World-Games: The Tradition of Anti-Realist Revolt*. New York: Methuen, 1987.

Norris, Christopher. *What's Wrong With Postmodernism: Critical Theory and the Ends of Philosophy*. Baltimore: Johns Hopkins University Press, 1990.

O'Barr, William. *Culture and the Ad: Exploring Otherness in the World of Advertising*. Boulder: Westview Press, 1994.

O'Leary, Noreen. "Worldwide Creative: McCann-Erikson: A Blueprint for Campaigns that Travel Around the World." *Adweek*. 31 Oct. 1994: 42–45.

O'Neill, Paul. "The Only Rebellion Around." *Life* 47 (30 November 1959): 124–25.

Poster, Mark. *The Mode of Information: Poststructuralism and Social Context*. Chicago: University of Chicago Press, 1990.

Postman, Neil. *Amusing Ourselves to Death: Public Discourse in an Age of Show Business*. New York: Viking, 1985.

Roberts, Elizabeth. "Bahamas Goes Back in Play." *Adweek* 21, 1994: 3.

Rothenberg, Randall. "U.S. Ads Increasingly Attack Japanese and Their Culture." *The New York Times* 11 July 1990: A1+.

Said, Edward. *Orientalism*. New York: Vintage Books, 1978.

Sanger, David. "Detroit Leaning on Japan, in Both Senses." *The New York Times* 27 Feb. 1995: A1+.

Savan, Leslie. *The Sponsored Life: Ads. TV. amd American Culture*. Philadelphia: Temple University Press, 1994.

Shi, David E. *The Simple Life: Plain Living and High Thinking in American Culture*. New York and Oxford: Oxford University Press, 1985.

Shorske, Carl E. *Fin-de-Siecle Vienna: Politics and Culture*. New York: Vintage Books, 1981.

Sloan, Leonard. "Realizing That the World Does Not Sing in Perfect Harmony, YAR Marches to Each Culture's Drum." *The New York Times* 17 Feb. 1995: D16.

Snell, Bruno. *The Discovery of Mind: The Greek Origins of European Thought.* 1953; rpt. New York: Harper & Brothers, 1960.

Stanley, Alessandra. "Presidency by Ralph Lauren." *The New Republic* 18 Dec. 1988: 18–20.

Thackara, John, ed. *Design After Modernism.* New York: Thames and Hudson, 1988.

Tillich, Paul. *Dynamics of Faith.* New York: Harper & Row, 1957.

Twitchell, James B. *AdCult.* New York: Columbia University Press, 1996.

Vaughn, Karen. "The Socialist Calculation Debate." *The Elgar Companion to Austrian Economics.* Ed. Peter J. Boettke. Brookfield, Vt.: Edward Elgar, 1994: 478–84.

Venturi, Robert, Denise Scott Brown, and Steven Izenour. *Learning from Las Vegas: The Forgotten Symbolism of Architectural Form.* 1972. Cambridge: The MIT Press, 1977.

Wallis, Brian, ed. *Art After Modernism: Rethinking Representation.* 1984. Boston: Godine, 1986.

"The War in Military Ads? What War?" *The New York Times* 8 March 1991: D1+.

"Why Is This Man Smiling? Thousands Cheer Burroughs at the Novel Convention." *The Village Voice* 11 December 1978: 1+.

Wicke, Jennifer. *Advertising Fictions: Literature, Advertisement, and Social Reading.* New York: Columbia, 1988.

Wilkie, W. L. *Consumer Behavior.* New York: John Wiley & Sons, 1986.

Williamson, Judith. *Decoding Advertisements: Ideology and Meaning in Advertising.* London and New York: Marion Boyars, 1978.

# Index

# About the Contributors

**Rebecca A. Chaisson** is a candidate for the doctoral degree in Social Work at Tulane University. She has an M.SW. from Tulane and a B.A. in biology from Xavier University.

**Mary Cross** is associate professor of English at the Florham-Madison campus of Fairleigh Dickinson University. She is the author of *Persuasive Business Writing* (Amacom) and of *Henry James:The Contingencies of Style* (St. Martin's). She is a former advertising copy chief.

**Walter Cummins** has published a number of essays and reviews, and his short stories have appeared in more than sixty magazines. He is editor-in-chief of *The Literary Review: An International Journal of Contemporary Writing.* A professor of English at the Florham-Madison campus of Fairleigh Dickinson University, he teaches courses in modern writing and communications.

**George Ellis** is with Advertising Research Corporation and is completing graduate study in psychology. His areas of expertise include the impact of physical appearance, international business, and market research.

**Michael B. Goodman** is director of the M.A. program in Corporate and Organizational Communication at the Florham-Madison campus of Fairleigh Dickinson University. He has written numerous articles and books, including *Contemporary Literary Censorship: The Case History of Burroughs' Naked Lunch* (Scarecrow Press), *Write to the Point* (Prentice-Hall), and *Corporate Communication* (SUNY Press).

**Martin Green** is chairman of the Department of English, Philosophy, and Communications at the Florham-Madison campus of Fairleigh Dickinson University, where he teaches courses in new communications technology and language theory.

**Donald W. Jugenheimer** is director of the School of Journalism at Southern Illinois University. He is the author of four books on advertising, including *Advertising Media: Strategy and Tactics,* and is a former president of the American Academy of Advertising.

**Harry Keyishian** is the author of *The Shapes of Revenge* (Humanities Press),and *Michael Arlen (*Twayne Publishers), and has edited *Critical Essays on William Saroyan* (Twayne Publishers). He is professor of English at the Florham-Madison campus of Fairleigh Dickinson University and director of the FDU Press and teaches courses in Shakespeare and in film.

**Roger Koppl** is associate professor of Economics and Finance at the Florham-Madison campus of Fairleigh Dickinson University. He has written numerous articles on the production and distribution of knowledge in society and on the history of economic thought.

**Elise Salem Manganaro** is associate professor of English at the Florham-Madison campus of Fairleigh Dickinson University. Born in Beirut, Lebanon, she has taught at the University of Hawaii and is the author of a number of articles examining Middle East literature.

**Chester St. H. Mills** is chairman of the Department of English and Print Journalism at Southern University of New Orleans. Born in Manchester, Jamaica, he is a specialist in comparative literature and the author of a forthcoming book about writing.

**Judith Waters** is professor of psychology and director of the M.A. program in Psychology: Substance Abuse and Addiction Studies at the Florham-Madison campus of Fairleigh Dickinson University where she teaches consumer psychology and behavioral research. She does research and corporate consulting on the impact of physical attractiveness on social and economic outcomes and has discussed her research results on network and cable television.